LOOKING AROUND

Mississippi

SOME MORE

WITH WALT GRAYSON

SIT BACK AND RELAX.

Turn off the TV. Walt Grayson is about to guide you on yet
another journey into the heart and soul of the Magnolia State. As you will
discover in the pages of this book, some of the best of Mississippi lies beyond the
beaten path. Walt will show you places you've never known and remind you of others
long forgotten. Along the way, he will introduce you to the folks he meets,
generous souls eager to share a good story with Walt — and with you.

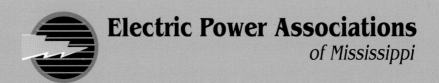

Electric Power Associations
of Mississippi

*A network of twenty-six electric cooperatives serving more than
715,000 members with affordable, reliable electric service*

www.epaofms.com

VALUE. Values.

The subjects of Walt Grayson's writings and photography reflect Mississippi's rich, diverse culture and its complex history. Yet each one shares a common theme: Life is good in a state where traditional values are revered, shared, and passed from one generation to the next. Mississippians just can't help caring for others, speaking openly and honestly, and working together for the good of all.

These same values helped ignite a grassroots movement in the 1930s that literally revolutionized life in rural Mississippi. In the midst of the worst economic depression this country has ever known, rural Mississippians came together to form electric power associations for the purpose of obtaining electric service for their homes and farms.

It was a bold move for an impoverished people. But the movement succeeded, driven by the will and the vision of its founders.

An electric power association is a not-for-profit electric cooperative owned and controlled by the people who use its services. By becoming members of a local electric power association, rural Mississippians demonstrated the traditional value of self-help to obtain a needed service that no one else would provide.

Founding members created a form of electric utility unlike any other. They crafted bylaws based on time-honored values: democracy, solidarity, equality, and accountability.

They knew that, whatever the future may hold, electric power associations would thrive if their fundamental values were solid and true.

Their vision proved accurate. Today, electric power associations collectively serve about 85 percent of the landmass in Mississippi.

Twenty-five electric power associations distribute electricity to residential, commercial, and industrial members. One electric power association generates and transmits wholesale electricity to eleven of these associations for distribution to their members.

Electric power associations:

- Serve more than 715,000 members (including some 618,000 residential members);
- Deliver electricity through more than 89,000 miles of line; and
- Employ more than 2,700 Mississippians.

Although an electric power association is an independent, locally owned utility, it benefits from being a part of a nationwide network of electric cooperatives.

This network serves a ready source of manpower and equipment during outage emergencies.

It takes a highly trained work force using advanced technologies to distribute safe, reliable, and affordable electricity in today's world. But no technology could improve upon the traditional values under which electric power associations have operated for more than seventy years.

Electric power associations...

Partners in the
Heart of Mississippi

Welcome to a state in which families are celebrated, children are cherished and neighbors are friends. Welcome to a state that respects hard work and humble gratitude. Welcome to a state that offers many scenic sites and historic landmarks.

Welcome to Mississippi and its electric power associations—partners in the heart of our great state!

Twenty-six electric power associations serve more than 1.7 million Mississippians and 85 percent of the land area of our state. Though we were born in mostly rural areas, we now serve

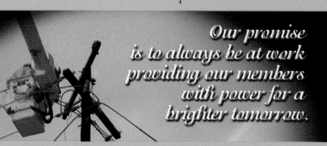

Our promise is to always be at work providing our members with power for a brighter tomorrow.

in many of the state's more populous areas. This partnership brought all the benefits of comfort, convenience, security, and productivity to the heart of Mississippi.

Electric power associations continue to strengthen our partnerships with the people and communities we serve. This close connection has created a legacy of value and values that we work hard to renew every day. Each electric power association is an inspiring example of neighbors, as partners, working together to make life better in Mississippi. Our employees are especially committed to the future of each person calling Mississippi home.

We are proud to have played a pivotal role in the growth and economic development of Mississippi. From our humble beginnings to the unlimited potential of the future, our highest responsibility is to provide dependable electric service at the lowest possible cost for our member-owners.

It's a public responsibility we take seriously. But it's also a personal commitment we take to heart because our future, like yours, lies in the heart of Mississippi.

The family of electric power associations is proud to publish the second edition of *Looking Around Mississippi*. Who better to take us on this journey than Mississippi's well-known storyteller, Walt Grayson.

We trust this book will encourage you to look around Mississippi and enjoy the beauty of our historic past, and the exciting promise of our future.

Michael Callahan

Executive Vice President/CEO

Acknowledgments

I AM FINISHING UP THE TEXT of this book while sitting in the dining room of our friends Larry and Chola French's old plantation house, "Montgomer," way back off a road, off a road, off a road in extremely rural Claiborne County. Thank-you to the Frenches for letting us borrow their peace and quiet to do a final collate. And thanks to their son, Leyland French, for tossing me the key to the gate and the house and insisting I come here in the first place.

A huge thank-you to my sister, Ermie, for proofreading the manuscript. I can never repay you, Ermie, so I won't even try.

As a matter of fact, all of my brothers and sisters, Linda, David, Ermie, and Robert, are inspirations to me. In our own way, we've all subtly challenged each other through life.

Thank-you to my wife Jo for having the patience to watch the Soap network for the past three days while we've been here at the plantation putting a book to bed. I PROMISE this is the last page. And thanks to you also for going out on the road on all these trips with me to begin with, and then letting me tell about our adventures.

As far as a dedication for this book, it goes to our kids, Jason, Keri and her husband Bryan, Tammy and her husband Brad, and all the grandkids. You'll meet them all in the following pages. Thank-you for helping us decide we needed to run away to the plantation for a few days.

And thank-you to the fans of *Look Around Mississippi* and *Mississippi Roads* for allowing me to be the one to do this job. This is YOUR book, too!

JACKSON DAYBREAK. Mark Twain went on and on about how beautiful the sunsets were in a town in Illinois where he once lived. As an aside, he added that he understood there were also wonderful sunrises, but he never saw any. My man! But I was up at daybreak one day, so I thought I'd better record the event in photography. No telling when that will happen again.

MS LAURA was put over her grave in the Kosciusko Cemetery by her grieving husband so he could see her from their house nearby. After she was placed, it was said that he could never make himself look at her. A descendent told me actually, by the time the statue was finally delivered, having been made in Italy, the husband had remarried and wasn't ALLOWED to look.

Walt Grayson

1·10·06

LOOKING AROUND
Mississippi
SOME MORE

with WALT GRAYSON

THE
DONNING COMPANY
PUBLISHERS

TITLE PAGE PHOTO CAPTIONS

LATE BLOOMERS. My favorite flower, the spider lily, will surprise you by growing and blooming between yard cuttings in late August and September.

PEARL RIVER CHURCH CEMETERY can cast enchanting spells on visitors when the time of day and the weather and the light are just right.

DELTA BAPTISTERY. Effective place to put it, just beside the cemetery. Candidates know which fork of the eternal road they've chosen after coming up out of the water.

THE CHAPEL OF THE CROSS in Madison County is as shrouded in lore as it was in fog this winter morning. There are ghost tales and lingering stories of lost loves associated with the church. It was built in 1848 and was a part of the Annandale Plantation, and looks more like it should be on an English moor than in Mississippi.

OPPOSITE PAGE

TRI-TRUNK TREE. Undoubtedly, this tree had a terrible accident when it was young, overcompensating to overcome it for the rest of its life. Ghosts are said to be those who won't give up and let go after death. Guess we'll find out someday.

Copyright © 2007 by Walt Grayson and EPA Foundation Inc. of Electric Power Associations of Mississippi

The Donning Company Publishers
184 Business Park Drive, Suite 206
Virginia Beach, VA 23462

Steve Mull, General Manager
Barbara Buchanan, Office Manager
Pamela Koch, Senior Editor
Amanda D. Guilmain, Graphic Designer
Derek Eley, Imaging Artist
Scott Rule, Director of Marketing
Tonya Hannink, Marketing Coordinator
Neil Hendricks, Project Director

Electric Power Associations of Mississippi
Michael Callahan, Chief Executive Officer
Ron Stewart, Senior Vice President
Debbie Stringer, Editorial Support
Mark Bridges, Graphic Support
Jay Swindle, Marketing

Photo on page 4, Brad Barr

Library of Congress Cataloging-in-Publication Data

Grayson, Walt, 1949-
  Looking around Mississippi some more with Walt Grayson.
    p. cm.
  ISBN 978-1-57864-447-6 (hard cover : alk. paper)
  1. Mississippi—Social life and customs—Anecdotes. 2. Mississippi—History, Local—Anecdotes. 3. Mississippi—Description and travel—Anecdotes. 4. Grayson, Walt, 1949—Travel—Mississippi—Anecdotes. 5. Mississippi—Pictorial works. I. Title.
  F341.6.G735 2007
  976.2—dc22

                          2007026637

Printed in the United States of America at Walsworth Publishing Company

Introduction

IT'S ALWAYS EASIER FOR ME TO WRITE the middle of whatever it is I'm trying to write than it is for me to come up with the beginning. I know where it is that I want to end up. I just can't decide the best place to plug in to get to it.

I saw a flock of migrating white pelicans rising up from the Barnett Reservoir one morning. In an ascent surprisingly graceful for so awkward-looking a bird, the flock swooped up slowly into the sky and started making a wide circle. Once, twice, three times they went around and then, as one, they headed off toward the south.

Those pelicans remind me of the way I start to write something. I circle around a few times until I get my bearings and then I'm off.

And I know where it is I want us to be off to: visiting more places around Mississippi. Although we covered quite a bit of territory in the first book in this series, *Looking Around Mississippi with Walt Grayson*, I still know of some more places I'd like to see, and I've heard more good stories I'd like to pass along.

In addition, we've had more road adventures ourselves while traveling to shoot stories for the *Look Around Mississippi* and the *Mississippi Roads* TV series. Stories that you might find as amusing as we did. Well, they're funny NOW, at least. Some of them were even funny at the time. Well, funny to the rest of us, maybe not so much the person directly involved. STILL not funny to them, some of them.

But the mishaps are a part of the fun. And having fun is what Jo and I have decided we want to do for the rest of our lives if at all possible every day. Both of us have had enough un-fun from life. And we try to remind ourselves to live above the moment in those instances when one of us has had enough and is poised to clutch the other's throat. The path of least resistance sometimes is to give in to aggravation rather than to try to rise above it. (Especially for Jo. Not me, of course.)

STARS AND STREAKS decorate the sky over Brandon one clear winter morning. When conditions allow contrails to be this visible, rumors fly that we are being gassed. Whoever starts those rumors has seen too many crop dusters.

Sometimes it really does seem that the enjoyment of the moment has to be purposefully sifted from the stress of it in order to find it.

For instance, high gasoline prices, especially right after Katrina, took the smile out of the miles on all those trips we made down to the coast to produce the Katrina DVD for WLBT and the follow-up stories for *Look Around* and *Mississippi Roads*. But now, we have great memories of the people we met and admire their courage and fortitude, and we wonder how they are getting along every time we go back in that direction.

At other times, the most fun in a situation is just getting it over with. For instance, a few weeks ago, we had to spend three nights out on the road as we shot two half-hour TV shows and four feature stories. That's a lot of work thrown into that short a time span. The major lesson we learned from that weekend: don't stay in any motel that has "airport" as a part of its name, no matter the rate. We had planes taking practice-bombing runs at us all night, every night.

Then, when we finally did get back home, our cat was in heat and went from room to room singing opera. I'd have rather had the airplanes. At least there were periods of quiet between them.

But as we say, when life gives you lemons, choke somebody! Or, maybe better, when you have a problem, solve it. I will have the great satisfaction of solving one of our problems when I take our cat to the vet in just a little while to have its state of being altered. Jo's still not sure what to do with me, however.

Actually, we (not just me and Jo, but all of us, I'm convinced) really don't appreciate that we are enjoying doing what we do as we do it. For instance, for Jo and me, sometimes, about the only acknowledgment we give the actual pleasure that we derive from driving all over creation shooting stories and then hurrying back home and editing like mad in order to meet another deadline is that we must like this sort of thing or we wouldn't do it.

OH, *THAT* WAY! Vapor trails over Ocean Springs one morning remind me of having to circle a few times to get bearings.

THE DAYDREAM SPOT. An antique wooden desk sits beside a cabin window overlooking a secluded wooded area in Madison County. Sitting here, I could daydream a lot easier than I could work.

STAMP OF APPROVAL. I get a kick out of seeing the creative way people decorate their mailboxes. If I have time, I stop and snap a picture. This one is dressed up for the Fourth of July at Shrock House in rural Madison County.

RED BLUFF. You never know what's under your feet. Here in Marion County between Monticello and Foxworth, an eroded hillside reveals some of our hidden color.

HATTIESBURG HIGH SCHOOL. The boys had an entrance on the other side. An arsonist did major damage to the historic old building in May of 2007.

COURT ADJOURNED. When Prentiss County split into thirds, each new county built itself a new courthouse, leaving this one at Jacinto deserted. It was sold to a salvage company for $600—but rescued in time.

And it is only just every so often that we remember to actually take stock and remember that we DO like what we do. Usually, all that reflecting comes in those rare, quiet times when there are no planes buzzing us or cats serenading us, or when nothing else distracting is going on. And life being what it is, those moments don't manifest themselves very often.

But in those scarce instances when we come to ourselves, we remember the wonderful gift that life is while it is happening.

I have made the comment to Jo more than once that I don't want to wait until I am eighty years old and wake up one morning and realize we really were having fun right now while we are doing all of these TV stories and riding all of the roads. We need to know it now. Every day. And to recognize that you are enjoying life while you are living it is a rare gift indeed.

It's so feebly easy for me to fritter away my time longing for the good old days. Or to imagine how wonderful things are going to be someday after I attain some vague life goal, beyond the threshold of which I have convinced myself "living" can begin. But what is most elusive is to be cognizant of the right-now pleasures and enjoyments that are going on continuously but are often overshadowed by the insistent demands of everyday living. And I know those things are happening every day we live. Because after all, isn't it the memory of those past pleasures and enjoyments that were there all along but unrecognized at the time that makes us yearn for those good old days?

BILOXI LIGHTHOUSE. The building stood through Katrina. This shot was taken a few years before the storm.

MENDENHALL COURTHOUSE. There's a bunch of Mississippi towns that have the look of a Mayberry to them. With Courthouse Square keeping sentinel over Main Street, Mendenhall is one of them.

What do you think it is we crave so much from back then except the sanitized memories of the goodness that is life that finally float to the surface after all recollection of the details of the proximity of moment-to-moment living have dissolved? But instead of recognizing those pleasures in the present as we are living them, what do we do? Concentrate on the close proximity of the pressures of the day. Or we spend our "nows" alternately regretting the past or fearing the future. The former of which it's too late to do anything about. The latter, too early. And in the process, we overlook the only real existence we have, and that is what is going on right now.

It is always going to be "right now." So if we can't learn to enjoy life right now, then we will never be able to enjoy it. The past is a memory; the future is a fantasy. Right now is the only time we have in which we can snatch the "carpe" from the "diem."

So maybe that's a good direction for us to head off in. Head toward discovering the pleasure and enjoyment of life as we are living it. Not as things used to be in the good old days or as it could be someday but as it is right now.

And then, just for my benefit, let me set all of those wondrous discoveries down in print in this book so I can pick it up and re-see them every time I start getting shortsighted and drift from living in the moment back into lamenting yesterdays or being terrified of tomorrows. That's what we'll try to discover in the stories in the pages ahead. Extracting living out of life today.

Plus, we'll throw in some pictures for good measure. Ready for a Mis'sippi Odyssey? Me too! Let's go!

TINY WORLDS grow at our feet. Don't get in such a hurry as not to notice.

ST. PADDY'S PARADE, JACKSON has grown into one of Mississippi's most popular events. Sweet Potato Queens from around the nation come here to show off on Capital Street.

Dear Friends,

The pages of this book with images seen through the remarkably talented eye of Walt Grayson serve as great reminders of why we are so proud of our state. Walt is a beloved Mississippi storyteller whose words and photographs in this second edition of *Looking Around Mississippi with Walt Grayson* are sure to enlighten and entertain.

These depictions capture the uniqueness of Mississippi in all of its awe-inspiring beauty. Many of the images portray the same sort of resilience and self-reliance demonstrated by the courageous people of this state in the aftermath of Hurricane Katrina, the worst natural disaster in American history. Every day I see wonderful people caring for each other and working hard to build Mississippi back better than ever, just as they work to rebuild their own homes. The indomitable character deeply rooted in our culture cannot be shaken, not even by a natural disaster of epic proportions.

We are happy to share our culture, which really is what this book is all about. From rolling hills to Delta flatlands, from Coastal sands and the high water mark of Hurricane Katrina to towering pines, Mississippi beckons you to take a closer look. Imagine a walk in the woods or a glass of sweet tea with a neighbor. Mississippi is the place that personifies the Southern spirit of hospitality and heritage; it's the place Marsha and I will always know as home.

Whether you live here or are just visiting, I think you'll treasure this look around Mississippi.

Sincerely,

Haley Barbour
Governor

Foreword

My last year in Mississippi I had the unmitigated pleasure of working with Walt on his long-running show, *Mississippi Roads*. The reason I joined him as co-host was simple: he asked me. Since I'd become a southerner, *Roads* had been a favorite program of mine. Because Walt told me about it, I had been to the watermelon seed spitting competition in Mize (forty-two feet), the Neshoba County Fair (of course), the German Festival, and a dozen other out-of-the-way places that, not only did I thoroughly enjoy, but also gave me stories of my own to tell.

Working with Walt was even better. He knows where everything is, he knows where everything *used* to be, he probably knows where all the bodies are buried, but he's so crazy about the state I doubt he'll ever tell. Unless it makes a good story.

Wherever we went to tape the show, people knew Walt. They rushed up to him, followed him around wanting him to film their special place, tell their story. Once I was known to be on *Roads*, I was always getting stopped in the street or the women's locker room or the Kroger's produce section. The first words were usually: "Will you tell Walt . . ."

Walt. Not Mr. Grayson or even Walt Grayson. Walt.

Taping a show can be grueling, particularly in the heat of July and August, but I never saw him cut anyone off. He didn't just pretend to be interested and listen to be polite or keep his audience. He really was interested. He really did listen. Walt is a fanatical collector of stories. His wife, Jo, and I became good friends over the months I was on the show, and we used to gossip behind Walt's back when he was doing a solo piece on camera. (The price of stardom, Walt.) Jo told me of their weekend trips, Walt with a camera close at hand, waiting to catch just that moment of light over a rice field in the delta or the last wisp of a haunt slipping around the corner in an antebellum mansion, Walt standing in blowing dirt and cotton to talk to a kid on a bicycle, a kid that looked like he might have a story, Walt nearly driving into a ditch because clouds behind winter branches etched a perfect sky.

Walt is an excellent writer, photographer, and performer. Seldom do all three talents come together in one man, but that isn't the spark and the spirit that makes his second book as much fun as his first. What imbues Walt's work is a wonderful mix of obsession and love. He obsesses over words and work, and he loves people, images, and, most of all, his home state of Mississippi.

Nevada Barr

SCIPLES MILL is perhaps the last operating water-powered gristmill in the state. Edward Sciple has the doors open every weekday except during deer season. Near Dekalb, Kemper County.

EARTH HONOR. Frost John Kelly in Utica must have been a saint among men while he lived to have the glorious epitaph he has on his stone. Wonder who wrote it? I don't know who I'd trust to write mine. Or who would trust me to write theirs!

FRANKLIN MARKER. A marker with a moral. Here's the story of two friends who went into business together and dissolved friendship and partnership and life on earth for one of them in a duel. Another lesson, careful how you die lest it be engraved over you.

THE MIDDLETON CEMETERY is all that is left of a once busy town until the Yankees burned it. The cemetery wouldn't even be here had it not been for the Winona Lions Club sifting the hillside and cutting the brambles and putting it back like this.

Contents

SOUTH BEACH ON HORN ISLAND has opposite connotations than those associated with Miami in the category of the number of people you'll see there.

RED, WHITE AND BLUE. The popcorn tree, cloud, and deep sky of fall.

Katrina

NO DOUBT HURRICANE KATRINA IS THE BIGGEST THING to impact Mississippi lately. We all helplessly watched the satellite and radar images of the monster storm as it worked its way across the Gulf of Mexico and directly onto our coast.

The day before the storm hit, we were in Jefferson County doing a story about the anniversary of Salem Missionary Baptist Church. The church has roots running back 225 years, making it the oldest congregation in the state.

On our way to the church, Jo kept saying she felt like she should stay at home and get ready for the storm. I confidently assured her that we wouldn't need a thing at our house two hundred miles inland. After all, I had lived in Jackson when the remnants of Camille came through in 1969. So I knew all about these things. And my lights didn't even go out. So if Camille was no problem, how could Katrina be one? After all, everybody knows Camille was the storm of all storms.

But still, Jo had her doubts.

Looking back, I can't believe that I was so positive almost to the point of being condescending when Jo went on and on about really needing to be at home at the grocery store stocking up. But I wasn't the only one to be fooled by the magnitude of Katrina.

We attended our church service and shot our story and decided to go on south to Natchez and get something to eat. We noticed the traffic getting heavier and heavier the closer to town we got. So heavy, in fact, that both lanes of Highway 61 South were clogged and at a standstill from where Highway 84/98 intersects with it.

So we doubled back and took the newly completed Natchez Trace into town. It had been within the last year or so that the seven- or eight-mile section from Highway 61 into Natchez had been completed and opened. It was still so new to me I wasn't sure where it came out. But there was no traffic on it, and it put us into position to ease through downtown and on to the restaurants on the river.

KATRINA DOLL, PASCAGOULA. Like so much else that had been loved and cherished before, Katrina left this doll as a lost orphan in the street.

Leaving, we discovered that Highway 61 northbound was clear. Only the southbound lanes were jammed. What was happening was that people were trying to take Highway 84/98 and cross the Mississippi River at Natchez. And where 61 and 84 and 98 all were the same road was where the traffic was impossible. It was so bad that people were hopping out of their cars and taking pictures of the jammed traffic with their cell phone cameras.

We flipped on Public Radio and found Gene Edwards already on the air with all sorts of official evacuation information and taking calls from people with either questions or personal observations. From listening, we discovered the New Orleans area was being evacuated, and traffic coming north on I-55 was being diverted westward at Brookhaven toward Natchez to cross back into Louisiana so people could find shelter from that point. Hence, our traffic jam.

So I called Gene on my cell phone and went on the air with the suggestion that some of those people stacked up in Natchez might want to turn around and go north on the relatively empty lanes of Highway 61 to Vicksburg and cross the river there. Or take the Trace to Jackson and reenter I-55 for Memphis or just get a room in the Capital City (where all would be safe and warm and dry, implied).

NATCHEZ TRAFFIC JAM. Granddaughter Taylor snapped this shot of heavy traffic coming into Natchez the Sunday before Katrina hit the coast and New Orleans. Since Katrina, many people have moved to Natchez from New Orleans and the coast.

RAIN DANCE. Video still image shot in our yard of trees being stretched to their limit during Katrina, 180 miles inland.

By now, Jo was convinced more than ever that she should have stayed at home and gotten ready to hunker down. I kept my amusement to myself.

I do remember one call in particular Gene had on the air from a man in Pass Christian. They were chatting about the state of the weather at the time on the coast and what the caller could see of preparations being taken by his neighbors. Boarding up windows, bringing in the trash cans and lawn furniture, things like that.

Then Gene asked him where he was going to ride out the storm. Right here, the caller replied. Why, after all of the warnings, would he want to stay there? "Oh, this house made it through Camille," he answered emphatically, as if to question the need for the question.

Over the next days and weeks, I remembered that call and often wondered what happened to that guy and his house.

A few weeks later, we were at the ruins of Beauvoir shooting some video for the Katrina DVD for WLBT and ran into Jeff Lawson, news anchor at WLOX in Biloxi. Jeff was doing a live shot for their 6:00 p.m. news. Jeff and I got to talking about the storm and how it surprised so many, including me, because so many people were using Camille as a barometer, logic being that whatever survived Camille could survive anything.

Jeff told me that the mayor of Biloxi had observed that Camille probably killed more people in August 2005 than it did in August 1969 when it hit, because people judged their chances of survival by how they fared in Camille. And if they did okay in 1969, then they discounted the warnings about Katrina, thinking none of that could apply to them because their home or wherever they were holing up was hurricane proof.

As a matter of fact, people only really started taking Katrina seriously after Governor Barbour got the weather service to word the warning that another "Camille-like" storm was approaching.

All I can say is I am glad I didn't own a waterfront home on the coast that had survived Camille because I probably would have tried to ride out Katrina in it, thinking I was invincible. It got bad enough at our house in Rankin County north of Brandon, well inland.

BEAUVOIR SCORE BOARD. Down but not out the spray-painted sign is saying. After Katrina, there were just two National Landmarks left on the coast: the Biloxi Lighthouse and what was left of Beauvoir.

CAMILLE MEMORIAL. The engraved names of the dead and missing following the coast's previous worse storm wasn't treated with much respect by Katrina, rubbing it in as to which was biggest and baddest.

All was calm that Sunday evening when we got back from Salem Church and Natchez. Network shows were running as usual on TV, as I recall. Jo was still antsy, however. But I was still sure we'd have no problems.

"Just wait and see," were the words that I said too many times that day and night before Katrina struck, words that would be mimicked back to me as if spoken by a parrot over and over for days as we struggled to get gasoline and water and ice and food.

But clearly, we weren't hit as hard as the coast. We had an inconvenience where we lived, but our lives weren't changed forever.

Monday morning, August 29, 2005, dawned blustery in Rankin County. By 8:00 a.m., the deteriorating weather conditions had my full attention. Thankfully, Jo didn't start saying "I told you so" right away. She waited until the opportune moment when it would achieve the full impact, and then continued the barrage until—well, I started to say when she stopped saying it, but I don't think she has, yet.

For a while Monday morning, conditions were really kind of nice for August. We turned off the air conditioning and threw open the screened windows on the side porch. Enjoying the balmy conditions, we smugly remarked about how much electricity we were saving. We saved a bunch more by that afternoon when the lights went out and stayed out for much of the rest of the week.

Monday noon is one of the three times a week I am supposed to be on the set at WLBT to introduce one of my *Look Around Mississippi* stories. Driving in, I was well aware that conditions had worsened to way beyond what Camille ever did in Jackson. Trees swayed, traffic lights danced, stop signs were doing the shimmy, limbs were falling, and rain was coming in horizontal sheets. And we were still hours away from the height of the storm.

I made the remark to Wilson Stribling, anchoring the Noon Report that day, that I thought we had a new benchmark. I told Wilson that it was beginning to look to me as if Katrina would replace Camille as the storm of our lifetimes. That was still hard to believe at that point. I don't

BRANDON DAMAGE. Destruction reached far inland. The steeple of the Brandon Presbyterian Church was blown off the building. Brandon is over 150 miles from the coast. Locations even farther northward had worse damage than this.

FRIENDSHIP OAK. This photo was taken some years before Katrina. The legend says anyone who walks hand in hand under the oak will remain your friend for life. The tree survived Katrina.

BAY ST. LOUIS looked more like it had been hit by an earthquake than a hurricane.

GLOOM OF RAIN. I was going to do a story about the mail carrier fulfilling her duties during the flooding rains of Katrina until I realized I didn't remember the exact wording of the Postal Service motto. And the Internet was down, so I couldn't look it up.

WILD RIDE. Video still of our wind surfer trying his hand in the Barnett Reservoir during Katrina. This was probably the last fun anybody had for weeks.

know that I really fully believed it at that moment, just as in 1969 it had been difficult to set aside Betsy during the early hours of Camille.

Reports from the coast, which was getting hit with the full brunt of the storm at that time, were sporadic and sketchy, like trying to keep up with a battle as it was progressing—the fog of war. But what we were hearing made our hair stand on end. Could it be true?

I went back to the house after my Noon Report duties, not really knowing what I needed to do. As the lights started flickering that afternoon, Jo and I got the camera and headed out to see what we could see. We spotted a mail carrier soaked to the gills trying to deliver mail in the driving rain. I thought that might make a good story, a mail carrier living up to the motto of not letting the gloom of night or the rain and stuff (at that point I realized I really didn't know the Postal Service motto) keep her from her appointed rounds.

Driving on around Fannin Landing Circle to the Barnett Reservoir, we spotted a guy trying to windsurf. We shot some video of him from inside the car with the window on the downwind side rolled down. The wind was just too strong for a good ride. The sail kept blowing out of his hand every time he tried to get it upright. Usually he went with it. Once he looked as if he were a flag flying from the mast as his hands gripped the bar and his feet went straight out in the wind—didn't last but a second or two, then he was back in the water. The party ended when a deputy stopped and honked his siren a time or two and made him get out of the water.

The reservoir looked rougher than I had ever seen the Gulf. The thought then passed through my mind, "What MUST be going on down there?" The actuality of what was really happening at that moment "down there" far exceeded anything I was imagining, however.

I had really started dreading Katrina the night before when I turned on the Weather Channel and they said the barometric pressure in the eye of the storm at that time was then lower than that of Camille. And the head of the National Hurricane Center had already telephoned the mayors of Pass Christian and Bay St. Louis and warned them the eye was probably going to make landfall in their area and to evacuate immediately.

That is when a dull sinking feeling began to settle over me. I couldn't fathom Pass Christian and Waveland and Bay St. Louis being directly in the path of the storm. Just the Thursday before, Jo and I had been in Bay St. Louis shooting a story and doing some shopping.

The story was about the Right-Hand Coast and how mid-state revelers were beginning to discover places to the right of Highway 49, places such as Long Beach with the Friendship Oak on the campus of the University of Southern Mississippi facility there. (Friendship Oak made it, by the way. I don't think the campus has yet reopened.) And visitors were also enjoying quaint little villages like Pass Christian and Bay St. Louis with its Second Saturday Art Walk when the artisans of the town pull their wares to the sidewalk for a sale and a party.

There was a certain candle shop (they sold more than candles, but it was a candle shop, too) that Jo loved on the main street of Bay St. Louis. She'd always come away with things to turn wine bottles into oil lamps and scented candles for the side porch and stuff.

I liked one of the antique shops within spitting distance of the beach. We've been looking for a dresser for our bedroom since Keri, my daughter, decided the one she let us use while she was away at college—one I paid for, mind you—was really hers, and she'd like it back whenever we could find a replacement. The search takes on more urgency at some times than at others. And this particular time the search was on.

So Jo found the perfect dresser at our little antique shop. But I was dead tired. We had spoken at a cable television operator's convention the night before and then shot the Right-Hand Coast story that morning. And I didn't feel like rearranging all of the equipment in the back of the Tahoe to make room for a dresser. So I told Jo we'd come back the next week and get it and maybe take a day or two off so we could play for a while. We'd get the dresser then when we were not working.

I had even found an old edition of Shelby Foote's three-volume Civil War series. But I didn't get that, either. I figured since we were coming back for the dresser the next week, we'd get it all then.

As we were leaving Bay St. Louis, we drove through the neighborhoods with all the quaint seaside cottages they had there and played our game of picking out which one was ours, not knowing we'd never see them or the town ever again as we had just seen it.

By now, the afternoon of Monday the twenty-ninth, as we were shooting video of our windsurfer, Jo's candle shop would have been completely inundated along with the antique shop. And my books and the dresser and everything else we had intended to come back and get the next week would have been washed into the Bay of St. Louis.

We weren't thinking about that at the moment. When we got back home, we discovered our lights were down for the count. And Jo was already getting stopped up from all of the stuff being blown in with that "wonderful" breeze. Trees were down; power lines were down. One hundred percent of our electric power association was in the dark by then. And remember, we are two hundred miles inland.

Tuesday, August 30, dawned clear as a bell. All creation looked sort of like a drunk waking the next day from a blackout brawl pitched the night before. Everything was a mess. But the sun shone brightly, and the air was dead still.

And it was HOT! There was no electricity to power an air conditioner—or power the refrigerator or coffee maker either, for that matter.

I rigged a power inverter to the battery on the riding lawn mower and shot off an email to my sister just before the phone service died. I had a generator in the garage somewhere, which I had most recently used as a sawhorse. The last time I had tried to crank it, it wouldn't run. But I had put off fixing it until later.

By the way, there is an oil pressure sensor on generator motors that, over time, goes bad just

---

MONEY SAVER. Video still of how we really snookered the power company at our house. The breeze was so cool the day of Katrina we turned off the air. The following spell without electricity until the state could be rewired wasn't so pleasant.

HARD TIMES were in store for the Hard Rock Casino, wracked by Katrina on the eve of its grand opening.

sitting there and won't allow the thing to start because it perceives there is no oil in the engine. I managed to find it and pulled the wire off it, and we finally had enough power to make coffee.

There were extension cords running all over the house. The small TV in the kitchen was plugged in to a power inverter hooked to a jumper battery sitting on the stove. The first thing we saw was Coyt Bailey and Joe Root's footage of the aftermath on the coast from Skycopter Three.

Jo and I both were thunderstruck. My eyes got misty, my lips pressed tightly against each other, and a lump welled up in my throat as we watched and saw there was no more coast.

The helicopter was trying to show the damage to the yet-unopened Hard Rock Casino and managed to fly just enough over the Biloxi small craft harbor to show the slab where McElroy's restaurant had been. We had just eaten there less than a week before.

As breezy and pleasant as the previous night had been, it was just as hot and still that next night. Even with gasoline at a premium, we needed to get some rest. So I pulled my little Geo Tracker into the side yard, cranked it, and let it idle all night as it powered an inverter that ran a fan upstairs in our bedroom.

We were uncomfortable but realized we were infinitely better off than people on the coast. That reality was brought home to us time and time again over the course of the next few days as we started making our way southward to do stories about Katrina—what it did and how it affected people.

So many people had seen the Skycopter Three shots of the coast and had requested copies of it that Dan Modisett, WLBT station manager, asked me to take that footage and collect other stories and edit it all into a DVD for the station to sell. All of the profit would be donated to hurricane relief.

Over the next few weeks, Jo and I visited every community on the coast from Pearlington to Pascagoula. The damage was the same everywhere. It was more extensive in places, but anywhere by the water was totally gone. In some places it only went inland a few blocks, other places a mile or so. But everywhere beside the water for a hundred miles was gone.

We decided to take the two younger grandchildren with us on some of the trips we took so they could see the damage firsthand. Hopefully, they'll never see anything like Katrina in their lives again.

We never take them on long trips together anymore, however. Not since it was my bright idea to take them with us to Gatlinburg on vacation about a month before Katrina hit. At that time, the youngest, Emily, was five and Taylor, the older, was twelve. I told Jo they'd love Gatlinburg and the Smokies. And they did.

GRANDDAUGHTER EMILY went with us on one of our trips to the damage area. We took photos she could show in kindergarten the next day.

EMILY, TAYLOR, AND JO and seven states from the top of Lookout Mountain in Chattanooga less than a month before Katrina hit back home. The kids were good when we stopped. So we stopped a lot.

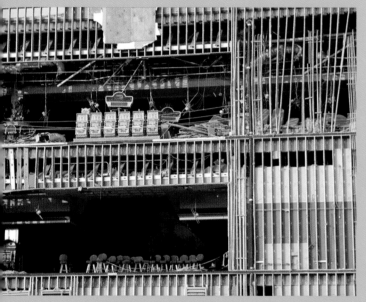

CAMILLE MEET KATRINA. We always passed the boat that Camille lifted across Highway 90, amazed at the power of the storm. We couldn't drive down Highway 90 from the east after Katrina because one of the casinos the storm had floated loose was straddling the roadway. That's it there in the background.

GULF COAST RISING. The full moon rises over the industry and will of the Coast as pilings also rise from St. Louis Bay replacing the old bridge with a bigger and better one.

LUCK RAN OUT for not only this casino barge dislodged by Katrina, but also for the historic hotel and antebellum home crushed beneath it when it landed.

PALM TREE AND D'IBERVILLE. Sometimes, it was surprising what withstood the storm winds and surge.

RING IN THE OAK near the Church of the Redeemer has withstood another storm. The church building didn't fair nearly as well. One survivor told Jo as I was shooting this shot, "If you ever see The Weather Channel broadcasting live from your town, you had better get your butt on the road away from there."

But the ten-hour drive to get there and back was something I hadn't anticipated. And I KNOW Brad, our son-in-law, put Emily up to it. We were no more than five miles away from the house when she started asking, "Are we there yet?" (That's why now, when Emily spends the weekend at our house, I make sure to feed her sugar just before she goes home.)

And then she and Taylor would get into it. "Make her stop looking at me!"

At one point, the five-year-old had run the twelve-year-old off the back seat and onto the floor and wouldn't let her get back up. I got tickled by her spunk but couldn't let on.

Now, they really did like Gatlinburg. Gatlinburg means shopping. That's why I try to get us embedded in traffic in Cades Cove for as long as I can when we go there. When you are stuck in Cades Cove in the mountains, you aren't spending money in Gatlinburg.

After a few days, we were almost back home from our excursion. The two girls were going at it again. About the time we were driving through Carthage, having had my fill of back seat bickering, I leaned over to Jo and told her, "Well, we've done this. We don't ever have to take them anywhere together ever again."

Taylor was with us the day we went down to shoot video of Bay St. Louis. Gasoline was still sporadic at best on the coast, so every time we went down, we would fill up in Hattiesburg on the way so we'd have plenty to get us back home if we couldn't find any on the coast.

Downtown Bay St. Louis was a shock. Sand dunes swept the main street where all our favorite shops had been. A car was piled up on top of a heap of debris at the door of the Masonic Hall.

Tony Thornton, a highway patrolman friend of ours from back home, was on duty in downtown Bay St. Louis and told us to be sure we noticed the debris line as we went back under the I-10 overpass at Highway 603. We got to the overpass, and I was looking along the concrete uprights where 603 goes under the interstate trying to see a water line. Taylor was the one who spotted it, way up at the top of the ramp about three feet under the I-10 bridge. I guess the water must have been at least fifteen to twenty feet deep right there. And this was five miles in from the Gulf.

We were riding around near the beach where there was enough roadway left to drive on, trying to find anything recognizable or where it used to be, when Jo said she needed a restroom.

You don't know how addicted to civilization you are until you have to do without it. NOTHING was open for business as usual in Bay St. Louis. Pretty much the whole town had been flooded by the storm surge from Katrina. Shopping center parking lots were Red Cross disaster relief staging areas. There were no service stations or fast-food restaurants or any other place that might have a restroom open.

There were porta-potties all over, however, set up for the convenience of volunteers coming into the area to help out. We were passing by one of them for the third time when Jo decided that she WOULD use it, after all.

I pulled over to the shoulder of the highway and stopped. Cars and trucks were zooming past us, shaking our vehicle as they went. Jo was thinking out loud when she said, "Gee. I hope that thing doesn't blow over."

WHITE CHURCH, BAYOU CADDY. Camille floated it off its foundation blocks. Katrina sent it sprawling across the road. Loyal parishioners vow to put it back right, as all of the coast shall be.

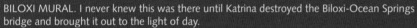

BILOXI MURAL. I never knew this was there until Katrina destroyed the Biloxi-Ocean Springs bridge and brought it out to the light of day.

BILOXI FISHERMAN STATUE. It's a summation of the coast, knocked off its foundation by Katrina.

RAINBOW BARN PRE-KATRINA. The barn has been a familiar sight for decades on I-55 south of Hazlehurst.

RAINBOW BARN POST-KATRINA. As with many other landmarks, Katrina stole the sole identity that was the Rainbow Barn's alone and branded it with her own mark.

FIRE DOG SALOON. Katrina let the dogs out.

At that, Taylor nearly busted a stitch laughing. She thought that was the silliest idea she'd ever heard, that a porta-potty could blow over. Then, for the rest of the day and all the way back home, Taylor would spot something and blurt-giggle, "I sure hope that cement mixer doesn't blow over. I sure hope that hospital doesn't blow over."

That scene from Caddy Shack where Rodney Dangerfield says to someone, "Now you know why tigers eat their young," came to my mind after a little while of Taylor's "hope-that-thing" drivel.

A day or so later, Jo and I were back on the coast mopping up the remaining video that we needed for the DVD. It was the same day that Hurricane Rita was coming in.

In Pearlington, we talked to one man who told us about riding out the storm at his house. The water was rising almost to the top of the walls inside when the eye of the storm came over. During the calm, he floated outside tethered with TV antenna wire and kicked out the boards above the door at the end of the garage and hoisted himself, his wife, and two dogs into the attic just before the winds whipped back up from the opposite direction.

He declared he'd never try to ride out another. If Rita started heading this way, he'd be off to Hattiesburg.

Later, on the beach at Pass Christian, it was beginning to look as though Rita might be headed our way. The sky and water were leaden. Clouds whipped inland from the Gulf, and whitecaps dotted the surface as far out as you could see.

Sand was blowing in stinging gusts across what was left of Highway 90. I had set up the video camera and was shooting eastward down the highway, panning with the flow of the wind from the

RITA ROLLS IN to the west of where we were, in Pascagoula. What a deceivingly beautiful sunset.

IT CAN HAPPEN. Winds from Hurricane Rita toppled two porta-potties, satisfying Jo to no end that she had proof to show Taylor that it can happen and justifying Jo's inclination to always calculate any situation's worst possible scenario.

water to the dunes along the roadway. Suddenly, Jo said, "Give me the still camera. Quick!"

I handed her the camera and looked around to see what was so important that she wanted to take a picture. It was two porta-potties, blown over by the gusts of Rita. "I want to get a picture of this to show Taylor that it CAN happen!"

That was the last day we visited the coast for several weeks. We just had to go find other stories elsewhere. It was too overwhelming and sad, and we had to get away from it for a while.

But we'll never forget things like the acrid smell that was roughly akin to a garbage dump with a natural gas leak that permeated the whole coast for weeks. And of people in a daze with nothing left: no home, no car, no job. Nothing. And we will remember that no matter what we've experienced before and how rough it was, it can always be worse. So we won't take anything lightly again, because Katrina proved that ANYTHING can be blown over!

BAY ST. LOUIS BATHTUB. Houses and their contents were strewn all over the place by Katrina. No telling where the tub came from.

BAY ST. LOUIS STUMP. This huge mass of tangled roots was one of the deposits of the storm. Obviously it attained a status, noting the mayor's sign.

BILOXI STATUE. Before Katrina, you just had to know where this statue was in order to see it. After the storm, it's about the only thing in the area still standing.

SHOPPING CENTER. What was inside these quaint little shops in Bay St. Louis and Pass Christian ended up either way inland or way out in the Gulf. Little was left where it was.

39

Civil War

BY THE WAY, I FINALLY DID GET A SET of Shelby Foote's Civil War series. Jo picked it up as an early Christmas present while we were in Pass Christian signing books last November. I have set a goal to read it in at least no more time than it took Mr. Foote to write it.

It seems to me that interest in the Civil War has dwindled from what it was when I was a youngster. Of course, when I was young, Grandpa Grayson was still talking about how much better off the South would have been if they'd not shot Lincoln. You wouldn't believe how long it's been since I've heard that topic brought up as table conversation.

For me, there is an aura and a mystique surrounding the Civil War, even more now than I imagined it when I was younger and the old folks were still talking about it or when I was studying the war in history. The Civil War is the demarcation line between this nation's B.C. and A.D. Nothing has been the same after it as it was before. And what was before has been so romanticized and exaggerated or washed over by movies and novels written and produced by people who knew very little about what they were filming or writing, that the first mental images of the antebellum South we conjure in our minds nowadays have been so tainted by media that they are probably nowhere near accurate. Just as one example, personal bathing habits were such in the nation back in those days that, as a friend of mine puts it as he takes guests through his Vicksburg tour home, "If Miss Scarlet DID exist, you would have been able to smell her about as far as you could see her." No wonder they had so many magnolia blossoms draped all over the houses back then.

A century and a half ago, people sent invitations to funerals much as we send invitations to weddings today. And these invitations were bordered in black and had pale engravings of angels or shrouded figures or urns or other funerary images imposed over black, night-looking backgrounds. After already having read a great deal of Mr. Foote's account of that war, I envision the pages as I

THE RAYMOND CONFEDERATE CEMETERY isn't unlike any number of similar burial grounds in the state. It's a throwback to another place and another time that none of us, no matter how well studied, can really get a grasp on because too much has happened since then to weld the United States into a solidly united country.

read them as being encircled by those same types of foreboding images. It's all the death. Grant could lose about three thousand men over an hour's time and call it a good day, if he had inflicted more loss than that on the enemy. And he had some good days like that.

As I read about the great players of the war, even brought to life as they are in Mr. Foote's books, I still can't help but imagine them as if they were already posing for their marble statues, drained of life and enshrined while they yet lived. Most of them, in a sense, were posing for their statues. From generals to foot soldiers, they knew they were making history. Some were very concerned about how they would be remembered, or whether they would be remembered at all. Many knew a good showing in the field might lead to bigger things later—the White House, perhaps, as it did for Grant.

But it's the ghosts from that war that linger. Men drinking coffee around a campfire at sunrise, blown into eternity in bits and pieces before noon. And the generals used the men like cordwood. Chop a few hundred down ordering a mad dash across an open field, stack them aside, and send in a few hundred more to be cut down in their wake. Had to. Only way they knew to fight a war.

And the modern-day political and racial interpretations that have been imposed on the motives and outcome of the war are so erroneous they would be comical, if they weren't made a part of the policy and law and political correctness of today. These recent reinterpretations have left a scar on our part of the nation where no prior wound existed to such a degree.

But my mental pictures of the war and its participants are all filtered through the shroud of death. I can't read about what Lincoln was doing or saying without seeing him already assassinated. Every reference is draped in black bunting. Every word he says I hear knowing what end he is headed toward.

It's eerie. The war is all death, death, death. The whole thing played out in a mausoleum. So many people died. So many others came back home missing arms and legs. So much of the wealth of the South eroded away, went up in smoke, or was carried back up North in duffle bags.

CONFEDERATE MONUMENT, JACKSON. Just a little over a century and a half ago, Mississippi was part of another country. Slavery may have finally sifted out to be the biggest issue the war solved, but the monuments aren't to honor slavery. They just remember a time when we were somebody else and now we aren't, anymore.

Yet people today have taken on this ambivalent attitude toward the Civil War, or have shied away from it entirely as if it were contaminated. I think that comes from too many of our modern historians retroactively imposing modern motives into the minds of the makers of a war that took place in our great-great-grandparents' day. Grinding modern-day axes on a stone that old is ridiculous. Most of the issues modern scholars and politicians have come up with and assigned to the war, saying those are what they now believe the war was really fought over, hadn't even been invented way back then.

That, along with the so-called dumbing-down of America, leaves us a public hard-pressed to date the Civil War in its proper place on a timeline of our country's history, much less be aware of its actual causes and the real consequences of it that we are still living with every day in modern life.

It's too bad our Civil War quotient has slipped because we have so much related to it that still remains here in Mississippi. I don't know if the shrinking interest means students are not learning as much nowadays or if the war is really that politically incorrect and therefore PC people are shying away from it.

I'm with Arthur Davis, owner of the Old Country Store Restaurant in Lorman. Arthur, who is black, says he'd love to see a Civil War theme park created somewhere in the area. I asked him if he didn't think the subject was a little too sensitive to be broached. He said it's too late to get mad over

THE REASON FOR THE RUCKUS in most Mississippi towns wound up being whether the town had a railroad. This one in Iuka attracted all kinds of attention, North and South.

43

THE RAYMOND EPISCOPAL CHURCH to this day still has bloodstains soaked into the soft pine floors from those wounded at the Battle of Raymond in 1863.

THE OLD CAPITOL, JACKSON, is one of the few surviving buildings in the capital city that was standing before the Civil War. Speculation abounds as to why it and the governor's mansion and city hall and a few homes were spared. Best reason I can come up with, Sherman and Grant didn't want to burn them.

SHORT TRIP. Armies walked in Civil War times. Today, we zip in our cars. And the travel time between these county lines is no more than about eight seconds even if you are poking. Highway 25.

UNCLE HENRY'S, MOON LAKE, is more associated with Tennessee Williams than the Civil War. Williams, when he was a child riding along with his grandfather who was the Episcopal minister in the Clarksdale area, would have come here on parish calls with him. More historically significant, Uncle Henry's backs onto the Yazoo Canal on which Grant tried unsuccessfully to float an armada down to Vicksburg.

THE CANTON FLEA MARKET invites shoppers to invade the Madison County seat twice a year. Confederate General Joe Johnston and Union General Sherman were fans of Canton. But I don't think either could have withstood the barrage of bargain hunters that hit town every May and October.

something that happened that long ago. But we in Mississippi in particular ought to, instead, get rich over it. Why not? The past is past and isn't going to ever, ever change. Why not change the future, instead?

The shadows of the prewar South are still with us in the grand mansions in Natchez and Columbus and Holly Springs and other places. Battlefields are still preservable here in Mississippi.

Former slaves freed from Jefferson Davis's brother's plantation started the Delta town of Mound Bayou. Even the aftermath of the war set the stage for such things as Memorial Day, first celebrated here in Mississippi. There are, even still, a few elderly people living as of right now whose fathers were Civil War soldiers or whose fathers were slaves. I'm not kidding. I've talked to some of them. They were old, old men who married young, young women. And these children are getting on up there themselves, now.

I was asked to speak to a group of social studies teachers in Natchez recently. And, of course, the Civil War came up in the talk. I mentioned what I knew about my great-grandfather on Daddy's side of the family, Hiram Welch (Daddy's mama's daddy). He was one of the unfortunate soldiers who got quartered up in Vicksburg.

One story handed down over the generations was how, early on in the siege, Granddaddy Welch threw away a piece of moldy bread as uneatable. Then as the town ran out of food, he went back to where he threw it to see if he could find it again.

Mine wasn't a slaveholding family. Any kin of mine involved in the war fought for the same reason that so many other Southerners fought: because the Union army was down here. One of my cousins, Phyllis Harper, a historian and journalist in Lee County, made the comment that our family had enough "sense" all right, but we never managed to amass enough "cents" to be able to rub two dimes together. So much for being wealthy landholding gentry.

Speaking of Lee County, there's another Civil War story that I recall Mama telling about one of her grandmothers. As the Union army made a sweep through northeast Mississippi, a Yankee

THE WALTER PLACE, HOLLY SPRINGS, was built by Harvey Washington Walter. Since he owned the Central Mississippi Railroad, he wanted the finest house in town. His railroad attracted Union General Grant to Holly Springs, and Grant chose this fine house in which to quarter his wife and son while he occupied the town.

soldier caught the last chicken in her yard. She was a pious Christian lady, and the only cuss word anybody ever heard her say in her entire life was what she said when the soldier stole the chicken. She said that she hoped that damn chicken died. Later in the day, some of the kids found the chicken, discarded dead in a ditch not far down the road. The prayer of a righteous man (or woman) prevaileth much. Even when not puttest in the form of a prayer, exactly.

Guntown in Lee County has an unusual headstone in one of its cemeteries. I couldn't take you to it on a dare now; it's been so long since I've seen it. But several years ago, I got a call that a marker bearing the name of John Wilkes Booth had recently been erected over a previously unmarked grave in the middle of a family cemetery just outside Guntown.

The story goes that the man the Union army cornered and killed in the barn in Virginia ten days after Lincoln was shot was NOT the man they were looking for, John Wilkes Booth, although he was carrying Booth's papers in his pocket. Some say the army was under such great pressure to capture the assassin that they just got somebody, anybody.

The Booth family was not allowed to see the body brought back to Washington from the barn in Virginia. Instead, Booth's surgeon was called on to identify the body. He remarked that Booth had an olive complexion and dark hair but the man he was to identify

TUPELO GUARD. For as much as we hear about Vicksburg, northeast Mississippi had its share of Civil War action, too. Corinth, Holly Springs, Tupelo, Meridian, and more.

JOHN WILKES BOOTH is supposedly buried beneath this headstone in a secluded cemetery near Gun Town. My interest isn't so much whether he is or isn't, but that somebody erected the stone. My brother Dave got this shot—proof I wasn't alone and left the gate open.

as Booth had more of a reddish-colored hair and was fairer skinned. Plus, the wrong leg was broken on the dead man. But the official version was that this was Booth. And he was buried in a secret grave and that was that.

But according to a Booth family legend, evidently that WASN'T that. Sometime afterward, a mysterious stranger started staying in the attic of the home of a distantly related Booth family in Guntown. He would come and go, but when he came, he stayed for several weeks at a time. He was only referred to as "Unk," and the children weren't allowed to discuss him with anybody. And he walked with a limp.

When I was doing a story about the headstone, I interviewed a descendant of the Guntown Booths who lived in Greenville. He told me that he thought the whole idea that Unk was actually John Wilkes Booth was hogwash. However, he did show me a gold cufflink that had belonged to the old man engraved with the initials JWB.

About six weeks after the John Wilkes Booth story aired, I got a call from an irate man in Memphis accusing me of leaving the gate open to the Guntown cemetery, allowing cows in the pasture to come into the graveyard and knock over headstones. I don't know why, of all the people who must have come in and out of that cemetery in the weeks since I had been in there, he figured I was the only one who could have left the gate open. I suppose he thought all TV reporters were idiots and didn't know how to close gates or doors or come in out of the rain.

Thankfully, I had witnesses with me, including my brother David, who snapped a few still shots of the headstone, as well as one of Guntown's history buffs who lived nearby—same fellow who took me to the cemetery to begin with.

I assured my caller that in my fifteenth summer, I had worked on my uncle's dairy farm long enough to learn two things. One: close every gate that you go through immediately; it just makes extra work when you don't. And two: that I didn't want to work on a dairy farm all my life. My agricultural career consisted of me going in circles on a tractor in a hayfield from sunup until sundown raking hay on good days. On rainy days, I was a pilot at the barn. Scrape it up and "pilot" over here.

Maybe that satisfied the caller or maybe he thought I was a liar as well as an idiot.

Is John Wilkes Booth really buried in Mississippi? Probably not. I don't know for sure that anyone was buried beneath that stone bearing John Wilkes's name. But it makes a good story. And the story isn't whether it's true or not. The story is that there is a headstone with that name on it in Guntown.

I've often told people I rarely check on the factuality of stories lest I lose a good story. Don Estes at the Natchez Cemetery nearly ruined a good one for me. There is a grave marker there that reads simply, "Louise the Unfortunate." Great embellished stories about Louise have been conjured up over the years, the best one being that she was a fallen woman of New Orleans come to ply her trade in Natchez Under the Hill. And it was only after she died that it was realized no one knew

BRANDON GATE. In places where North squared off against South a century and a half ago, tranquility hangs so thick now you can almost cut it. A Brandon pasture would have been active in the war but is pastoral nowadays.

her last name. So a benevolent minister purchased the grave marker with the simple epitaph that we see there now and placed it over her resting place.

Then one day recently, just before Don retired as director of the cemetery, he told me he had been going back over burial records and had discovered Louise's last name listed in a dusty old register. I told him not to tell anybody or we'd lose one of the best Natchez Cemetery stories we had.

Don is writing a book of his own about the cemetery. I can't wait to get a copy to see if he reveals the true identity of Louise.

Speaking of good tales I've never wanted to check the validity of, fearing it may not be true and I'd have to quit telling it, one such story concerns Ross Barnett's last campaign stop before being elected governor.

The way it was told to me was that anyone running for statewide office back then superstitiously made his last rally in Raleigh because Bilbo always made Raleigh the last stop in any of his campaigns.

Raleigh was one of the few, if not the only, county seats in Mississippi that didn't have a railroad. And in his speech, Mr. Barnett thundered, "If you elect me governor, I'll see to it that Raleigh gets a railroad!" At which, one of the attendees stood up and snidely asked, "Mr. Barnett. What on earth would Raleigh do with a railroad?" To which Barnett unhesitatingly replied, "SUE 'em!"

LOUISE THE UNFORTUNATE may not have been as unfortunate as we have been led to believe. But it could have been worse if they DID know her last name but chose not to use it on her headstone. But that's a whole 'nuther legend.

I don't dare check to see if it is a true story or not. I like it too much. And if it didn't happen, I couldn't use it anymore. By the way, Raleigh still doesn't have a railroad.

I told my group of teachers in Natchez that I never had to become an expert on the Civil War because I knew one. And he was always just a phone call away. Gordon Cotton has just recently retired as curator of the Old Courthouse Museum in Vicksburg. But for years, any time I needed to know anything pertaining to the Vicksburg Campaign or life along the river in general, or Southern lore, all I had to do was call Gordon.

I saw him just a few weekends ago at a cemetery cleaning and dinner on the grounds in Edwards. Last time I had seen Gordon before that was at a sacred harp singing and dinner on the grounds at Jordan Chapel in Warren County. Jordan Chapel (pronounced Jerdan) was designed and built by friend Hobbs Freeman. Before that, we were at a Methodist church homecoming and dinner on the grounds in Claiborne County. Gordon commented that it seemed to him the only places he saw me nowadays had food involved.

While Gordon labored away all those years at the Old Courthouse, I wasn't the only phone pal he had. Daniel Pearl, the *Wall Street Journal* reporter who was abducted in Pakistan and killed shortly after 9/11, earlier had been doing a series of stories about the Civil War for the *Journal*. Gordon told me that he and Mr. Pearl had become good telephone friends and often discussed more than just the subject at hand. In one of his phone conversations, Mr. Pearl revealed to Gordon that he did not believe in hell. To which Gordon shot back immediately without even having to think, "If there's no hell, then where's Sherman?"

That was a headline in the *Wall Street Journal* the next day.

JORDAN CHAPEL with its exaggerated height suggests that it was extracted from the pages of an enchanted storybook. Many pleasant times are had there from sacred harp singings and dinners on the grounds to Christmas carols shared among good friends.

OUR
MOTHERS

CHOCTAW, NATCHEZ STAIRCASE. Much of the antebellum splendor of Natchez survived the war simply because Natchez was not as strategic a location as places like Vicksburg. Why? No railroad at Natchez like at Vicksburg. Go see the war in Vicksburg. Go see the surviving Old South in Natchez.

THE CONFEDERATE WOMEN'S MEMORIAL STATUE in front of the new capitol in Jackson is just a reminder that the war went a lot further than to just soldiers. None were untouched: men, women, North, South, slave, free. We're still touched to a degree by the war today.

HOMESTEAD. A small percentage of families in the South were owners of slaves. Most came from small homesteads. Why did they fight? To protect those homesteads.

OXFORD CONFEDERATE STATUE AND COURTHOUSE. There are statues honoring Union soldiers on courthouse lawns up north. Only difference, their courthouses up there never swapped hands like ours did down here. Oxford was always tempting for the Union army up the road in Holly Springs.

Sherman left his mark on Mississippi during the Civil War. Supposedly, Sherman's often quoted comment that "War is Hell" was spoken in Jackson as the general watched a team of mules and two cannon tumble off a makeshift pontoon bridge into the Pearl River. The people who lived here could have better said it as Union troops and Yankee-freed prisoners from the state penitentiary, located back then where the new capitol building is today, ran rampant through houses, took what they wanted and burned the rest. Jackson mayor at the time, Earl Boyd, had to be put to bed after a Union soldier rode horseback through his yard on Jefferson Street bayoneting pigs just to hear them squeal.

There are not many parts of the state that didn't have at least some brushes with battles and skirmishes during the war. With the Union's strategies to capture major railroads, blockade seaports, and divide the South by retaking the Mississippi River, there wasn't too much of Mississippi that didn't qualify in there somewhere.

THE NEW CAPITOL, JACKSON, was built over the foundations of the old state prison. Grant and Sherman sprung the prisoners when they took the town in the Civil War. I guess they thought the pandemonium of loose convicts running wild through the streets could only add to the hilarity of watching the homes of unarmed civilians being burned to the ground.

Even the Piney Woods got in on the action with deserter Newt Knight forming his own band of men and hiding out in the Leaf River swamps and taking on any who would try to root him out, Union or Confederate.

Jones County where Knight lived wasn't a plantation or slave-holding area and really didn't see the need in leaving the Union. So when Mississippi seceded, the story goes that Jones County seceded from the secession, forming the Free State of Jones. (Another story you shouldn't check on too closely if you like it.)

Newt Knight didn't believe in the reasons for the war and stayed out of it until he was drafted. Then he served as a hospital orderly. Served until he learned that if a man owned twenty or more slaves, he was exempted from military duty. Knight resolved right then that it was a rich man's war but a poor man's fight and slipped back home to Jones County.

Other deserters began to join up with him until his small army totaled about a hundred men. They hid out in the swamps but managed to go back home enough to work their fields. And they raided supply trains going to and from Mobile.

The Confederate army sent Major Amos McLemore to Jones County to capture Knight and stop his nuisance raids. McLemore was from that part of the country and knew the swamps about as well as Knight knew them. On several occasions, McLemore nearly got his man and was becoming the most challenging adversary Knight had had to deal with up until then. So Knight decided to rid himself of the problem. One blustery September day, after an exhausting hunt, McLemore returned to the Amos Deason home in Ellisville where he was staying and was warming by the fireplace in his bedroom when suddenly Knight burst in through a porch door and shot him to death at point-blank range.

McLemore's body slumped to the floor before the fireplace, and his blood soaked into the soft pine boards. Years later, the bloodstain was still there and would not go away no matter how much

DOWNTOWN HOT COFFEE could be the capitol of the Piney Woods. Judy and Herbert Harper have a thousand things they can show you and a thousand tales they can tell you from the area's past when you stop by their store. Plus, the coffee is free after about 2:00 p.m. But then again, it's been on the burner since early morning.

THE DEASON HOUSE IN ELLISVILLE has its history and its ghost. Newt Knight secured himself a place in both categories by firing a single pistol shot in one of its bedrooms.

the floor was scrubbed. And on dark, stormy days, the stain just grew more pronounced.

So later generations of the Deason family installed another layer of boards over the original flooring so they wouldn't have to see the major's blood anymore.

The Deason home is owned by the Daughters of the American Revolution now and is open to the public. The room where Major McLemore was killed is still pretty much the way it was back then except for the new floorboards.

By the way, they tell me that the ghost of Mr. Deason comes and rocks in the rocking chair on the front porch of the Deason house, gazing out at the front yard where he is supposed to have buried his gold to keep it out of the hands of the Yankees. He died before he could retrieve it, and it has not been found since then. So on quiet, still days when the rocker on the porch starts to sway back and forth, back and forth, on its own, they say it's Amos Deason sitting there. And if you could only see where his invisible eyes were looking, you'd know where the gold was buried because that's what he keeps coming back to keep watch over.

There is an elementary school next door to the house now, and school children daydreaming out the classroom windows are sometimes shocked back to reality when they realize the rocking chair they are staring at on the porch of the house next door is rocking on its own.

I was doing a story about the Deason house and wanted to stage the rocker rocking to illustrate the part about Mr. Deason's lost gold. So I went out into the front yard and picked a place for my camera. What I had planned to do was frame my shot through the view finder and get my focus, then start the tape rolling and slip out of view and back up to the porch to nudge the chair and make it move.

But while I was still out in the yard zooming in to get my focus on the chair back, I saw in my viewfinder that the chair was already slowly rocking back and forth on its own.

Another place that still has bloodstains on the floor from the Civil War is St. Mark's Episcopal Church in Raymond. The church is right across the street from the Hinds County Courthouse. Both were pressed into service as hospitals during and following the Battle of Raymond early in the Vicksburg Campaign. There are still scars on the desks in the upstairs courtroom in Raymond from hasty amputations. Not long after Raymond, Jackson was taken by the Union with little

---

THE COURTHOUSE IN RAYMOND as well as St. Mark's Episcopal Church across the street are witnesses to the Battle of Raymond and its crude surgeries that left men who were whole and healthy that morning, either an amputee or dead by that evening.

RAYMOND ZINNIAS growing along the east wall of Raymond Mayor Isla Tullos's home on the square in Raymond is an example of former battlegrounds in Mississippi that have been tamed.

more than token resistance. Then came Champion Hill, arguably the most important battle of the Civil War. Here was Confederate General Pemberton's last chance to stop Grant in his tracks. And he had a pretty good shot at it if only he had had better cooperation from his subordinates.

At Champion Hill between Bolton and Edwards, America got its second birthday. That's where many experts say the Civil War was either lost or won depending on which side you are rooting for.

I am not historian enough to be able to project down through the ages what it might have been like had the South won its independence. Would we have wanted to have lived in the Confederate States of America (CSA)? I don't know. I often joke when pressed about the issue that I would be curious how much their car tags would have been.

Shelby Foote said in the interviews he did for Ken Burns's Civil War series on PBS that the war is the major factor in defining what we are as a nation today. A decade and change after that epic series, the disregard for that war also adds to the definition of what we are becoming.

I'm beginning to think that William Faulkner's observation about the past never being dead in the South, especially his reflection that it "isn't even past," is no longer true. Just from the way knowledge of the Civil War, or the desire to obtain that knowledge, is slipping away, I'd say if the past isn't dead, it sure is starting to grow colder.

KING COTTON. Slavery made cotton unfathomably profitable. In 1860, 60 percent of what the United States exported was Southern cotton. Slave-raised cotton made the whole country rich, not just the South. Hopefully some day soon, all descendents of that era, black and white, can settle the past and reap a future from what was sown by our ancestors, whatever their status was.

THE IUKA MONUMENT to a lost cause sums it up. We can't place ourselves in the continuum of history that was back then. The United States wasn't even a century old at the time of the war. And it was the first government of its kind in the world. Who knew if it was supposed to work? Who knew if the CSA didn't have a better idea? I guess they found out.

MISSISSIPPI INDUSTRIAL COLLEGE, HOLLY SPRINGS, was organized in 1905 by the Colored Methodist Episcopal Church to instruct African American young people in literary and industrial arts. The buildings are in desperate need of restoration today. The school represents the autonomy blacks attained in the wake of freedom won by the Civil War.

LAKE DEPOT. Thanks to Union General Sherman, we have this quaint Queen Anne depot in the Scott County town of Lake in central Mississippi. We'd have been stuck with the old antebellum one had he not burned it. Instead, we have this building that was built to replace it. Garden clubs in the area sold everything from pickles to pickup trucks to raise money to restore it.

Cemeteries

WE HAVE A BUNCH OF CIVIL WAR CEMETERIES in Mississippi. There is a string of them in the eastern part of the state in towns along the railroad running south from Corinth. The soldiers buried in them were wounded at the Battle of Shiloh, just north of Corinth in Tennessee, and were evacuated to the nearest town southward that could take them in. The ones who could recover, did. The ones who didn't make it are buried in those cemeteries.

Maybe the best known of these is the Confederate section of Friendship Cemetery in Columbus. During the Civil War, both Southern and Northern soldiers were buried here. In the years just after the war ended, most of the Union dead were moved from local cemeteries and were then reburied in national cemeteries in such places as Vicksburg and Shiloh.

But back before they were moved, a year to the day after the surrender of Lee's army at Appomattox Court House, the ladies of Columbus, Mississippi, took fresh-cut flowers to Friendship Cemetery to decorate the graves of the fallen soldiers of the South. After having done this, one of the ladies looked over and saw the bare graves of the Union fallen and thought it wouldn't be right to overlook them and not put flowers on their graves, too. So they did.

Word spread of this unbiased kindness by the ladies in Columbus. Eventually their act ended up as the topic of an editorial in Horace Greeley's *New York Tribune* that inspired Francis Miles Finch to write the poem "The Blue and the Gray," which was published in the *Atlantic Monthly*. And between the publicity generated by Greeley's editorial and Finch's poem, other towns and communities around the nation decided to start having their own Decoration Days.

Over time, as the United States fought other wars and more and more soldiers were brought home and buried, annual decoration days were still held but recognition and honor was expanded to include the latest soldiers too, as well as those of the Civil War. And the official date for Decoration Day was moved from April to the end of May when more flowers would be in bloom around the nation. And the name of the day was changed to what we still know it by today, the

THE ENTERPRISE CONFEDERATE CEMETERY is the final resting place for soldiers primarily from Texas. They had been hospitalized together at Enterprise.

more familiar Memorial Day. And it all started in 1866 in Friendship Cemetery in Columbus, Mississippi.

Now, in all fairness, there are probably more than a dozen places in the nation claiming to be where Memorial Day originated. Columbus, Mississippi, was given some degree of authenticity by a declaration of Congress many years ago. President Johnson went so far as to decree that Waterloo, New York, was the birthplace of Memorial Day. So there is some dispute.

But one thing that isn't in dispute is what the ladies of Columbus did that day long ago. Their action in placing flowers on the graves of the war dead of both sides led the way to the long path of healing between North and South. Word of their act of kindness ultimately permeated the whole nation and helped in the process of making it one nation again, in spirit as well as fact.

I am a fan of cemeteries. I like any of them I am able to walk out of. But the old ones with interesting headstones and interesting people buried in them are my special favorites.

AISLE OF HONOR. This cemetery in Kosciusko invites families to fly the flags that draped the caskets of their veteran loved ones twice a year. Veterans Day in November is one of those times; Memorial Day is the other.

Near the Confederate graves in Columbus is the weeping angel over the Tisdale plot. When I first saw it, I thought this was one of the most touching pieces of cemetery statuary I had ever seen. How sad it seemed, an angel slumped in sorrow over the passing of family members. I guess the irony is that angels are beings who belong to the "other side" where the dead are supposed to be headed. Seems angels would be happy to see someone they particularly liked or admired pass away because it would mean the spirit of the departed would be about to join them over there. But the implication of the weeping angel is that the vacuum left in the wake of some people's passing is just too empty to fill. And the sadness displayed in the statue was the angel's broken heart for those still alive and left behind who would, for the rest of their earthly lives, have to cope with the loss of the one who had died. Something like that must have been involved when Jesus wept at the tomb of Lazarus just before Jesus raised him from the dead.

Several years after I first saw the weeping angel in Columbus, we were just up the road in Aberdeen and discovered another weeping angel almost identical to the one in Friendship Cemetery. The same person, probably one of the expert cemetery marble sculptors in Columbus, undoubtedly created both pieces. It reminded me of how Jo is always worried that she'll show up somewhere and be wearing the same dress as someone else there. Dresses you can change. Imagine if you wound up with the same "unique" headstone over your grave as someone else nearby. Probably would make you want to die of embarrassment.

However, the most copied piece of cemetery art isn't a sculpture, it's a poem. I've had people email

MOURNING ANGEL, COLUMBUS is a touching piece of cemetery statuary. Its twin is just up the road at Aberdeen.

JESUS WEPT is the shortest verse in the Bible. For years, motorists were reminded of the tenderness every time they passed this sign on Highway 25. Widening the road took the sign.

me from all over the state and tell me to come see this eerie verse engraved on a headstone in a nearby cemetery. You've probably seen it or heard it:

> Pause stranger as you pass by.
> As you are now so once was I.
> As I am now, soon you shall be.
> Prepare for death and follow me.

Now, to me, this poem doesn't sound like what it's taken as, an attempt to warn passers-by of the brevity of life, as much as it sounds like sour grapes for being dead already and no longer being alive with the rest of us.

It reminds me of an episode back in my senior year of high school as we were nearing graduation. I was hanging out one afternoon after school with some of my friends in our neighborhood grocery store having a Coke when a man we all knew came in for a snack. And as he unwrapped his Moon Pie, he joined the conversation with us.

We seniors were bemoaning how long it had taken for the last twelve years of our lives to crawl by. But we were so relieved all of it was finally nearly over and we were almost out of school. Well, the guy snickered and said we'd be missing school in no time, which we couldn't begin to fathom at that point. And he went on to tell us, not only that, but how quickly the years would start to fly now.

ABERDEEN ANGEL. I had seen the mourning angel in Columbus many times before I ran across this one almost exactly like it Aberdeen. It's too good a sentiment to have only one. I guess I should have check death dates to see which came first.

"PAUSE STRANGER as you pass by" starts off one of the eeriest pieces of cemetery poetry you'll ever see. But the "pass by" part is the advantage we have over the one who is buried under the poem.

MERIDIAN'S MOST POPULAR MAN. The marker speaks for itself. And may already say more than I would have.

ERECTED
BY HIS
LADY FRIENDS.

LEE SHACKELFORD M.D

DIED
May 19, 1878,
AGED
44 Years 5 Mos.
And 4 Days.

I guess he was bragging when he told us that he was about to have his thirtieth high school reunion that summer. We winced as if we'd been shocked with electricity. The concept of being out of school for more than twice as long as we had been in it had never had any reason to cross any of our minds. It took us a second to absorb that a person could be that old and still be upright and have enough of his senses left to be talking with us. He added, just as we were wrapping our minds around the length of three decades, that it seemed to him like it had been no time at all since he was where we were, just graduating. And for us to just wait, we would be having OUR thirtieth reunion in the blink of an eye, too.

Here we were thinking we were just embarking on life, only to hear it was already nearly over. After cursing our young lives so, he left us with our mouths agape.

Suddenly, as in one of those Disney movies where dad and son, or mom and daughter (even a few where the family pet gets involved), change places, I started feeling older for the first time in my life, right then. A minute before I had been so young! Now, I had become the "old guy" who had just been talking to us.

Had he not said anything, no doubt all of us standing there would have caught on soon enough over the course of the ensuing years how "aging" and "swiftness" are used in the same sentence after a while. But we wouldn't have had to concede that cruel reality as high school seniors!

Pause seniors as you pass by,
As you are now so once was I.
As I am now soon you will be,
Prepare for becoming an old guy and follow me.

So every time I see a headstone with the "Pause Stranger" verse inscribed on it, saying in essence, "I may be dead but don't laugh, you're going to be right here with me in no time!" I think of that man and that conversation just before high school graduation.

PORT GIBSON TREE AND FENCE gives evidence of having been here a long time: the graves with the fence around them and the tree slowly absorbing the fence.

I'VE GOT YOUR MONUMENT. Look closely and you'll see that the monument is cracked and the pointing finger is slightly offset. If the departed beneath the monument was a crotchety old person, they may just leave it this way.

However, over the years I have come to realize something about the verse and about the passing of time in general. I've discovered that even though I may be on my way down that same path, I'm not NEARLY as far down it as those ahead of me are!

We did have our thirty-year reunion, eventually. But you know what? It wasn't until thirty long years later, after college and marriage and kids and a stab at a career or two. Know where the old guy was by then who had busted us when we were high school seniors? I don't either. But I expect to see his grave marker someday, somewhere while I am still able to walk away from it. And I'll be disappointed if it doesn't have that verse on it.

By the way, many people who've emailed me about this poem of doom swear it was original to their particular cemeteries. There's usually a legend attached to it about how it came to be written by the person buried there. The stories variously go that it was scrawled out by the dying person's finger dipped in his own blood gushing from a mortal wound inflicted by a duel/Yankee bullet/wild animal attack/or any number of other things, depending on the version of the legend you hear, just before he died.

I Googled the verse and discovered thousands of references to it spread out over many countries around the globe and going back a long time. The wording varies from place to place, but the meaning is the same: "Just wait, yours is coming."

There was one website that told of an additional couple of lines that someone had scratched at the end of the poem on

a headstone somewhere in Texas. The author had the right idea when he wrote:

> To follow you I'm not content,
> Until I know which way you went!

Wish I'd thought of that first. But even if I had, I'd probably not have gotten credit for it. As Mark Twain said, only Adam had the security of knowing anything he said couldn't be attributed to someone having said it before.

CEMETERY SHELLS. Conch shells are found as grave decorations in many places. Somehow they represent eternity. Maybe it's the cavity in the shell spiraling back into nothingness.

ENCLOSED MARKER. A tree grew over this cemetery fence post and was lost for no telling how long until the tree was cut down. I imagine the people who cut the tree were surprised to find the post in there.

DELTA GRAVE. I can't remember for sure where this grave decoration is located. Itta Bena maybe? I thought it was really elaborate and loaded with more symbolism than I could ever decode.

CRYSTAL SPRINGS SHELL. According to her writings, this was one of Eudora Welty's favorite cemetery markers. She photographed several other markers from this same cemetery.

There are other strange things on headstones. I got a call from someone wanting me to check out the grave of a person he said was obviously very evil who was buried in a cemetery near Union. The caller told me the headstone carving had a hand pointing downward with a chain wrapped around the wrist, apparently meaning this person was being dragged to hell for his evil deeds, directed there by the finger of God!

I don't know. We're pretty gentle with our dead here in the South. I've known of several awfully unsavory folks who instantly attained near-sainthood status just by dying. Mourning the just-departed seems to throw people into amnesia. The bad the deceased did in life goes into the coffin with them, and only their finer traits float to the surface to be remembered. Or, if they had no finer traits, their saintly mother or somebody else near to them was remembered in their stead. So actually having a derogatory insignia engraved on a headstone was something I'd have to see for myself.

Jo and I had spent the night in the cabin at Dunn's Falls near Meridian the night before and were on the way back home when I remembered the evil-handed headstone near Union. We had time, so we took the Highway 15 exit and went north to the graveyard at the church the caller had told me about, and we scoured the tombstones looking for the evil hand.

In the oldest section we found it. Sure enough, there was an engraving on this stone with a robed hand pointing downward and a chain. Only the chain wasn't wrapped around the wrist. The chain was sort of snapped with loose links dangling. I kind of figured this was what it would turn out to be. Loosely translated, the engraving means that God had selected the departed by pointing out the saint individually. He wants to bring the soul to heaven to be with him. And the chains holding the person to earth have been broken. Lots of hands point upward on grave markers and thereby do away with any doubt as to their meaning.

That's not to say we don't have some pretty strange cemetery art in Mississippi. For instance, there are graves of young twins in a cemetery just off the Natchez Trace near the Natchez end of it. The two young girls are buried side by side. On the top of one of the headstones is sculpted the

---

DUNN'S FALLS has just one rental cabin. After the gates close, the whole place is yours to roam at will.

TRACE TWINS. You have to go a long way to find cemetery symbolism this macabre. Cemeteries are for the living and are to somehow comfort those left behind in their loss. Dead doves just don't lift me up all that much.

BROKEN CHAINS and hands pointing downward have the same meaning as hands pointing upward: one pointing out the soul being sought, the other pointing the way for it to go.

likeness of two live doves. Atop the other are two dead doves. What were they thinking? Isn't it bad enough that the poor twins died? Must whoever commissioned these headstones conceive of cemetery art that will constantly throw the mourners into further perpetual depression every time they come visit the graves?

If you ever have a question about what a tombstone marking means, try to get in touch with Charles Sullivan at the Perkinston campus of Gulf Coast Community College. Charles is a good

friend and has photographed and researched more old cemeteries in south Mississippi than anyone else I know. In his classroom hang rubbings from the headstones of riverboat pilots with paddle wheelers on their grave markers. There's an engraved musket from a Revolutionary War soldier's grave. There's even a rubbing from the marker over where Stonewall Jackson's arm is buried.

Charles got me interested in trying to find some wooden grave markers he had discovered in a Piney Woods cemetery in Perry County. With a little luck, Jo and I found the markers as we took a "long-cut" on the way back home from the coast one Sunday afternoon. Using county maps, we managed to locate the church with the same name as the cemetery where the wooden markers were supposed to be. There was a graveyard behind the church, but no wooden markers. I figured they had been replaced, removed, or just rotted away since the last time Charles had seen them.

But about the time Jo and I, having written off the quest, were pulling out and were about to head back home, a man and his mother pulled into the churchyard, got out of their car with flowers in hand, and started toward the cemetery. Jo told me to go ask them if they knew of any other cemeteries nearby with wooden grave markers. That was too much like asking directions for me. So I told her no, let's just go on home. I think Jo had had just about enough of me by then that day, anyhow, so she popped open her door and before I could stop her, SHE was asking the couple about any other cemeteries where there might be wooden markers.

HAND IN HAND. Another gravestone that I can't remember exactly where it is. Maybe Jackson. If you ever start collecting grave art images, note where they are as soon as you can. You wouldn't believe how many cemeteries look alike later when all you have are tight shots of them.

They didn't know of any. But so they wouldn't think we were total nuts for looking for wooden grave markers, Jo rewound and played back an abbreviation of events that led to the search. Sometimes when you do that, you hope that something you inadvertently say in explanation is just enough of a hint to jog the memory of the person you are explaining everything to.

Sometimes I don't make myself clear when I am trying to ask for information and my daughter Keri will tell me, "Not enough verbs." So when Jo restated all the preliminary information to the son and his mother who were putting flowers on a grave behind the church, she evidently used enough verbs. Because as she explained we had been told we would find the odd wooden grave markers in this church's cemetery, a small flicker of recollection began to glimmer with the man when she mentioned the name of the church. He said what we might be looking for was the OLD cemetery where this church USED to be. I was using the wrong emphasis. I had asked the obvious—about wooden grave markers. Instead, I should have been asking about any other cemeteries nearby with the same name as the cemetery of the church where we were.

I was thunderstruck. This was the first time in my life that I'd ever seen rewinding and playing back get any response other than, "Sorry. STILL can't help you." (Which is why I stopped asking for directions years ago. I looked foolish for asking, and I never got any help, anyway. 'Course, maybe that's why I never got any help. I quit asking.)

The man and his mama couldn't give us directions to the older burial grounds, but they could

---

WOODEN MARKERS originated in the Carolinas and followed families migrating into the piney woods of Mississippi. I still think the reason for the diamond shape is that a circle is hard to cut with a straight saw if you don't know the trick.

take us there. Wasn't too far. By this time, a bank of afternoon summer storm clouds was beginning to build in the west. Ominous low rumbles of thunder echoed off the pines surrounding the lonely cemetery by the time we got out of the car. Then, there they were: the space-alien–looking, rectangle-bodied, round-headed wooden grave markers we'd been searching for.

Charles Sullivan said there isn't a mark on a grave or a shape of a headstone that doesn't have a meaning. He said from his research that the round heads on the wooden markers represented the spirit, somehow. But I noticed that not all the wooden markers in this cemetery had round heads. Some were diamond-shaped. Charles said he'd not run across anything in his research on diamond-shaped headstones, so he wasn't sure what they meant. But they meant something. Of course, I figure someone who didn't know how to saw a circle might have cut those out.

By the way, just as an aside to all the husbands reading this; if it looks like your wife

is going to jump out of the car and ask directions or something because you won't do it, when it is inevitable that she is going to do so anyway, quickly beat her to the punch and go on and ask for yourself, no matter how reluctant you are to do so. Because the humility you have to endure asking a dumb question of a stranger is over a lot quicker than all the "I-told-you-so's" that come if you hesitate and she gets the correct information instead of you.

As far as asking directions goes, Jo and I were looking for the house of one of her old friends in Belzoni a while back. And the directions we had been given might as well have been written in hieroglyphics for all the good they were doing us. Even when we found the big road we were supposed to be on, we never could find which little road it was we were supposed to turn onto. Jo said pull in and ask someone if they knew her, and if so, find out how to get to her house. Of course, as the man, I wasn't going to do any such thing. Besides, people don't tell complete strangers how to find a neighbor's house.

But it was already getting so dark that even the landmarks we had recognized so far were becoming hard to follow. So it was either stop and ask or just go on home. So Jo and I

GYPSY KING AND QUEEN. She died in childbirth at nearly age fifty. One lady said if it had been her, the husband would have preceded her. But he lasted many more decades. Those wishing favors leave offerings.

I GET IT.

OH BROTHER, A CEMETERY. When the Grogans in Madison County agreed to allow the filming of the cemetery and baptizing scenes for the movie *Oh Brother, Where Art Thou?* on their land, it was with the agreement that the cemetery would stay behind. The tombstones are made of Styrofoam, and the departed are the names of the crew working on the movie.

OH BROTHER CHURCH. No, this is not one shown in the movie, but surely it was inspired by the song the little girls sang that still won't dislodge from my mind, sometimes.

OH BROTHER, FINAL SCENE was of a railroad push car going under this wooden bridge at Edwards. If you like the bridge, get shots of it now. It will soon be replaced with a more functional structure.

OLD FAITHFUL sits at the foot of his master's grave in Jackson's Greenwood Cemetery. Good dog.

SITTIN' HERE AWAITIN' for something to happen seems to be the attitude of the lady in marble. Same feeling I get during funerals that are too long.

compromised. I pulled into a driveway, and she got out and asked.

Jo went to the door of a little cottage and knocked, then disappeared into the glow of the living room when the door closed behind her. A few minutes passed, and I was beginning to wonder what the delay was, when a man and a woman and Jo popped out the back door with Wal-Mart bags in their hands and headed for the backyard. I got out to see what was going on. By the time I went through the gate, the couple was already filling Jo's bags with ripe tomatoes and squash and new potatoes and lots of other stuff. As a bonus, they also knew Jo's friend and told us exactly how to get there.

I figure there is no place like Mississippi where you can pull in and ask directions of complete strangers, and they will not only tell you what you want to know but also give you a mess of butterbeans and a bunch of peas, too.

I turned to Jo as we were pulling out of the driveway and asked her if she thought it would be all right if we stopped at the NEXT house to ask directions again to see what we might get from THEIR garden.

I have tried to figure out what it is I like about cemeteries. It's a little bit morbid when you think about it. I mean, the place is full of dead people. But fact is, I never think about dead bodies being there except in passing. You never see them, after all, just their decorated plots.

However, we did get to see one of the dead bodies one time. It was in Natchez. Don Estes called me and told me that descendants of a family who had one of the crypts in City Cemetery were going to open it to check on the soundness of the structure just to make sure the old brick building wasn't about to cave in on its occupants. Knowing I am a cemetery fan, Don asked the family if it would be all right for me to poke my head in and take a look around while they had the crypt open. They said it would be fine as long as I didn't take any video or still shots.

The particular crypt was over 150 years old. The last person put in there was interred a long time ago, maybe over a hundred years. Then, as the crypt went into disuse, it slowly subsided into being just a part of the landscape of the cemetery, with crape myrtles growing up on its perimeter softening its lines, and the iron fence around it and its iron door rusting, fading from the harsh shiny black paint it had sported when it was new to softer shades of the deep reds and browns of nature.

I was really interested in seeing inside the crypt because I had heard rumors that there were bones on the floor. When my exploring friend from Mendenhall, Kirk Hill, went on an outing with his Model T club to Natchez one time, one of the places they toured was the cemetery. And

CROSS, BILOXI. Katrina didn't even spare the Biloxi Cemetery, doing major damage to the monuments there. This photo was snapped a few days before the storm as I was searching for death dates suggested by Charles Sullivan at Perkinston.

CRYPT WINDOW. Crypts with only heavy barred gates for doors are a little strange to me when you can look in and see the occupants. An occasional curious passer-by might give reason for a stained glass window. But why are there windows in crypts sealed as tight as King Tut's tomb? Maybe I'm too practical.

in their poking around, someone had dared to peek through the slats in the door of this particular crypt and saw what he believed to be bones. So when Don called and said I had an invitation to take an unobstructed look inside, I was excited.

Now, you may or may not know that the unspoken name for grandparents is "babysitter." It's just understood. And most times, grandparents are never asked if they'd like to baby-sit or if it's convenient, they are just given a schedule of when their services are required. Not that any grandparent who can lay proper claim to the title ever minds sitting the grandkids. As someone once said, if they knew how wonderful grandkids were, they'd have just started with them to begin with.

Well, Jo and I have four grandchildren. On the day we went to see the crypt, the three oldest, Michael, Kayleigh, and Taylor, were in school. The youngest, Emily, had just turned five and hadn't started kindergarten yet. So any time her parents (Brad, our son-in-law, and Tammy, our daughter) had to work, Emily got to ride along with Nana and Pops. And it turned out that the day we were to go peek inside the crypt was one of those days that we had Emily.

I hadn't thought too much about what to do if Emily wanted to look inside the crypt because up until then, Jo hadn't shown too much interest in going in there with all those dead folks, herself. So I just figured Jo would keep Emily occupied while I took my turn poking my head in.

When we got there, Don started filling me in on the background. The last time the door to this crypt was opened was forty years ago. Back then, the family had asked the cemetery management to go inside and just check on things. And when they went in, one of the cemetery crew found bones on the floor. What had happened was the Mississippi heat and humidity had evidently rusted out the bottom of one of those metal coffins that they used back in the 1800s, and the occupant was rather unceremoniously strewn all over the place.

The cemetery worker, having nothing better to put him in at the time, gathered up the bones, packed them into a wooden box, and put the box in a corner with the idea that something more fitting could be done for him later.

Well, now it was forty years later. And nothing better had been done with the poor fellow because no one had been back into the crypt since he was stacked in the corner all those long years ago.

Coincidentally, the same cemetery worker who had closed and locked that door for the last time forty years earlier was still working for the cemetery and was the one who was standing there with the key in his hand that day, forty years later, ready to be the first one back inside.

The lock clicked open instantly, to everyone's surprise. Didn't even need any oiling or anything. The door was a little stubborn to open, however. Settling over the years caused it to need a little jimmying with a crowbar at the bottom to jar it loose. And when it opened, its stiff joints moaned delightfully, like you'd expect the door of a crypt to sound.

The worker went in, then the descendants, then the structural architect, then Don Estes, and finally Don motioned for me to come on in.

There were several coffins on the shelves on the walls. I was expecting it to be stale and stuffy in the little room since it always stayed closed tight. But actually, there was a fresh faint sweet scent to the air.

The light, powder-blue plaster was corroding and falling off the brick inner wall in places. The massive iron door had little slits in it like the ones in the door in the famous painting of Jesus knocking that I remembered from our Sunday School books as children. The next thing I noticed was a small stained-glass window up high in the center of the back wall. I wondered whom that was supposed to be for.

Then, hardly recognizable at first, there in the middle of the floor was the box of bones. Except, over the forty years of sitting in a Mississippi sauna, the actual wooden box had long ago rotted away. But the bones were there in a tight pile. However, they were not where they had been left forty years earlier. The cemetery worker who had been the last one in the room back then seemed surprised, too. He reminded us that the last time he was in there, he had put the box in the corner. Now here they were out in the middle of the room.

As we were all wondering how that could have happened, I remarked that it seemed to me like the fellow whose bones we were looking at was trying to escape. He had already come out of his coffin and was making his way to the door. I told them, give him a hundred years and they wouldn't be able to find him!

I thought I had stumbled up on a sure 'nuff ghost story. I called my sister Ermie that night, and in my best movie narrator voice, I described how the bones had been left in a corner forty years ago but now, in a room unopened since then until today, they were in the middle of the floor. Ermie replied flatly, "Walt. You've been a weather man in Mississippi long enough to know what happened." I guess the long silence on my end of the phone gave it away that I didn't. "It rains heavily in Mississippi," she continued. "And over forty years, surely it would have rained enough at

LONG LIVED. I was searching for the oldest death date actually engraved on a headstone in Mississippi when I found this marker of a lady who forgot to die. I'm sure she did, but her date of death is not listed. Maybe she didn't want anybody to know her age.

THE OLDEST DEATH DATE on a tombstone in Mississippi is this one. The stone isn't nearly as old as the grave, however. And people have been dying around here for a lot longer, but they have no markers. Pascagoula.

some time or another to have flooded the floor of the crypt and floated the box."

I agreed that theoretically that could have happened. But it didn't! And slammed down the receiver. Mess up my good ghost story with logic?! The nerve!

But at the moment, while still in the cemetery, Jo was beginning to warm up to the idea of going ahead and taking a peek inside the crypt herself. So then Emily decided SHE wanted to look inside, too. I was caught in a dilemma. Should I forbid Emily to go in because she was too young to see the bones? (But for that matter, when exactly does one get old enough to see bones?) Or would it be more traumatic not to let her see inside, leaving her with the idea that there really are secret, awful things lurking in dark places in the world?

Besides, if I didn't allow her see inside, I'd be going against the modern grandfather guidelines that say, "Let 'em do whatever they want to do." Reminds me of my favorite quote by Sam Levinson. I vaguely remember him as a perpetually smiling, soft-spoken, pleasant personality on television from way, way back yonder. One of his observations on life says the reason grandparents and grandchildren get along so well is that they have a common enemy.

Besides, I thought back to the things my parents said I was too young to see or do when I was growing up. Most of what they were trying to keep me ignorant of I already knew about. Either that or it wasn't all that bad to begin with.

So I decided it probably would be better to let Emily go ahead and see the room than to try to protect her from it. At first, she just glanced around at the walls and the coffins. Then she spied the skull on the floor looking up at her with empty eye sockets from on top of the pile of bones. Her only comment was, "Pops, what happened to him?" I told her he was just having a bad bone day.

Emily was familiar with death by then. Sickness and death were what Jo and I immediately plunged into just after we married a few years ago. My mom died the day before our first anniversary. And then Jo's mom died five months later. So Emily had already been to a couple of funerals and understood the concept.

So after we left the cemetery, on the drive back home, Emily had some questions. "Why did they kill those people and put them in those little boxes in that little room?"

I explained that they didn't kill them; the people just died, like Nanny had. And besides, those weren't boxes, those were coffins. "What's the difference?" she asked. "Primarily price," I told her.

By the way, it turns out the bones we saw were those of a former Confederate soldier. I guaranteed Emily that she would be the only person her age to have ever seen a Civil War soldier in person. Admittedly, he was out of uniform at the time.

DEAR TO THE MEMORY OF… Beautiful cemetery markers are a thing of the past. Too expensive now, for one thing. Besides, memorial parks want your marker flat so they can run right over you with the lawn mower with no trimming. Perpetual care in no time at all.

Ghost Stories

LOGICALLY, AFTER THE CHAPTER ABOUT CEMETERIES should come some ghost stories. My only problem is, I have never really seen a ghost in person, or whatever. So I have no experiences of my own to tell other than of bumps-in-the-night kinds of stuff. That's not to say I don't believe in them. Or better put, I believe there are plenty of OTHER people who believe that ghosts exist. I've talked to several of those people over the years.

We were in Ocean Springs this past fall shooting a *Mississippi Roads* episode around the Peter Anderson Festival. Peter Anderson was the founder of Shearwater Pottery where his brother, Walter Anderson, gained much of his recognition.

At the festival we ran into Greg Harkins, who was displaying his famous handmade wooden rocking chairs. I was getting a little tired from walking from one end of the street to the other shooting video, so I plopped down in one of Greg's chairs.

Greg pulled up another rocker and sat down, and we chatted for a little while. Somehow, the subject turned to ghosts. Greg said that not too long ago an old man asked him if he knew why people don't see ghosts anymore. Greg said he didn't. And the man told him, "You can't see them when you're going seventy miles an hour."

Maybe that's it. Our lifestyle nowadays is moving way too fast for the spirit world to catch up. However, I know someone who has seen a wraith, which is the spirit of a person who has just passed away in one place manifesting itself to someone in another place, usually to say not to worry, they are all right but in a new place. I've talked to no telling how many people who have heard crashes in their houses when nothing has fallen. Footsteps overhead when no one is upstairs is a common phenomenon. I think I have heard distant undistinguishable voices myself.

Not many people I've talked to have actually seen a ghost. But some have. In Utica, a couple I was chatting with after I spoke to the Baptist Church senior citizens luncheon said Confederate soldiers have been seen in their kitchen. They walk right through the table and stand by the fireplace.

WINDSOR SUBDUED. If you don't believe in ghosts, then go to Windsor. You'll not see spirits of dead people, but the centuries will whisper to you in the forlorn breezes of the Old South.

Mrs. Snow, owner and restorer of Waverly Mansion between West Point and Columbus, told me about the ghost of a little girl who is often heard calling for her mama. In all her years at Waverly, however, only once did Mrs. Snow actually see the girl. The four- or five-year-old child was standing on the staircase of an upper floor. And Mrs. Snow said as she watched, the little spirit just turned smoke-like and vanished.

The "Evil One" did the same thing at King's Tavern in Natchez. He's been seen along with Madeline, who was employed at the tavern in its early days and who is also the original owner's alleged mistress. Madeline shows up so often she should still be on the clock.

My closest ghostly encounter so far was in King's Tavern several years ago. It was near Halloween, and I needed a ghost story. And I had heard the tales of Madeline and how she worked at the tavern back in the 1700s and perhaps had more duties than just wait tables, duties that Mrs. King did not approve of.

Well, one time while Mr. King was away on business, Madeline disappeared, never to be heard from again, until a chimney was being repaired a century and a half later and a skeleton was found.

ANDERSONS AT SHEARWATER. Jim Anderson and his son, Peter, carry on Shearwater Pottery in Ocean Springs. Jim's dad, Peter, founder of Shearwater, is in the photo on the wall. The old photograph had just been rehung, having been removed for Katrina, the day we shot this shot.

GREG HARKINS. The master craftsman has enough commissions to make chairs from cherished trees blown down by Katrina to keep him in the shop for years. Telling ghost stories is just a pastime.

KING'S TAVERN. Jacqueline Stephens gave me this photo from her Natchez ghost files. Jacqueline takes walkers on a ghost tour of downtown Natchez at night. The smoke in the photo was not visible to the eye but showed up in the flash shot. Some say these are spirits.

A dagger was found along with the skeleton. Since then, Madeline has manifested herself in person, as a shadowy figure in photographs, and in other ways, always when you're not expecting anything.

My friend Scott Kelly was with me to do the shooting, and I was just along to get the story when I went to Kings Tavern for my Halloween ghost story. The owner of King's Tavern, Yvonne Scott, told me about the time a psychic came wanting to try to contact Madeline. Yvonne said the little guy started gyrating and vibrating and getting so excited that the workers were way more afraid of him than they had ever been of the ghosts.

He stood at the foot of the stairs in the tavern that leads to the dining room up above and spotted Madeline at the head of the steps. "There she is, there she is!" he sputtered and started following her up. "She's beautiful," he went on, describing her waist-length blonde hair and light blue printed dress with small green flowers. He followed her up and up, as she went past the dining room, on up past the bedroom above the dining room on the next floor, and then on up into the attic over the bedroom.

The steps to the attic go from the floor to where a section of the ceiling has been cut out and one end of it hinged. You push up on the other end and walk on up into the attic.

The psychic crept up the steps to the attic door. He pushed it open and started on up. He got about halfway in when he stopped and slowly eased himself back down and quietly closed the door above him.

As he got off the steps, he told Yvonne that there were three entities in her building. Two were friendly, but the third was the beast. Yvonne told me at that point she was about like everyone else, she didn't know whether she believed in ghosts or not. But when someone tells you the beast is in your building, you want to know what to do. So the psychic gave her the sage advice, "Whatever you do, don't upset the beast."

Well, when she told me about the beast and the attic, I wanted to go see the attic right away. So just as soon as we finished the interview, I was first in line up the stairs past the dining room, then the bedroom, and finally to the trap door to the attic. I slowly went up the steps and eased up the attic door. No one had told me the door was counterweighted with a couple of those old iron

THE GRAND OPERA HOUSE, MERIDIAN before it was restored and became the showplace of the Riley Center. Back in those days, spirits were as likely as not to be encountered on lonely treks above the shoe store at street level as one climbed into the bowels of the cavernous deserted building above.

RATLIFF SUNSET. I snapped this late one day after visiting the family burial grounds at Oak Grove Cemetery at Ratliff. Whenever I bump into people who have heard of Ratliff, I automatically figure I am kin to them.

CAMDEN CHURCH. Someone said that the most haunted places are theatres, hospitals, and churches. If you see this one ever again, it will be a ghost. This building was torn down shortly after it was used in the movie *A Time to Kill*.

THE CROSSROADS IN CLARKSDALE is where Robert Johnson is supposed to have sold his soul to the devil in exchange for fame. I guess it worked. He's famous and so is the crossroads. 'Course he's dead, too. I'd have taken a little less fame and a lot more living.

window sash weights like they used to put on wooden windows. So as I eased open the door, these two arms dropped down on either side of me, and I raced down four floors onto the sidewalk in about two seconds.

After I realized what had happened, I sheepishly went back in and told them I had forgotten something. (My nerve!)

But we went on up into the attic and didn't see a beast. There was a pretty-good-sized air conditioning unit up there. But no beast.

And we came back down and shot pictures of the bedroom. By the way, there is a perpetual warm spot on the bed. I've felt it. So has Taylor, my granddaughter, as well as one of her friends who went with me to Kings Tavern on a more recent trip.

By the time we got to the dining room, below the bedroom but just above the tavern, it was beginning to get late, and we had shot no exterior video. I had my camera in the car and told Scott that if he would finish up with the interior, I'd go get my camera and hose down the outside.

So I left Scott, and a waitress who had attached herself to him, telling him about all the times she had seen Madeline, in the dining room as I went down the stairs to go outside and get my gear. But as I was walking through the tavern room below, I saw the fireplace and the chimney where the skeleton had been found, and I knew we had to get shots of that because finding it was central to the story. So I zipped to the car and got my camera and came back inside and set up to get shots of the fireplace.

And even though I was in the tavern room all alone, I wasn't afraid because I could still hear Scott and the waitress's muffled voices up above my head and the floorboards squeaking. I went to the north wall of the tavern, and the floorboards over my head squeaked there. I went to the south side of the room, and the muffled voices and squeaking floor followed me. So I figured Scott was getting thorough shots of the dining room. And I was relieved I wasn't alone.

However, my sense of security evaporated when I happened to pass by a window and glanced out and saw Scott and the waitress standing outside. I thought I'd quickly go out and join them. I asked Scott, if they were out here, then who was up above my head doing all the talking and all the shuffling in the dining room? Scott shrugged and said, "I don't know. We left when you did."

Thinking I might catch a ghost, I raced back into the building and started up the stairs to the dining room. Then thinking I really MIGHT catch a ghost, I had second thoughts about going on

MY ORB! Way up there in the branches of what I was told was the hanging tree on the lawn of the Adams County Court House, I snapped what ghost hunters call an orb with my flash digital camera while we were taking the Natchez Ghost Tour. Some people get these things all the time. This is my only, so far.

MISTY MORNING, BRANDON. We don't have time to visit our dead like families used to. Consequently, we don't tell our youngsters, as we were once told, how all these people under these headstones are kin to us. And how that makes us a part of something a lot bigger than just our individual self, with the implication that we need to act like it and not let all these folks down.

up. But I had already been flushed out of the building by a couple of window weights, so I couldn't back down now.

When I reached the top of the stairs, the dining room was dark. And when I flipped on the light, no one was in there. Including me. It doesn't take me long to check out the paranormal.

Now, that's about as close as I have ever come to experiencing a ghost. So I'll keep doing ghost stories as long as it doesn't get any worse than that. However, if I ever DO see one, I'll probably switch over and explore UFOs after that.

There is this one story that has been handed down through my family for a couple of generations. It isn't a ghost story exactly, but it's the next best thing to it. And it fits here better than anywhere else.

Way back, the custom of the day was to sit up with the dead. If a relative or a neighbor passed away, they didn't haul the person to the funeral home to be displayed there. The duty of the funeral director back then was to fix the body up and then bring it back to the house, where friends and family would come and pay their respects until time to take the deceased to the church for the funeral. Someone always stayed up with the body overnight.

There was an elderly neighbor who passed away in my grandfather's community many, many years ago. The old man and his wife had just one child. Their boy was grown by the time the daddy died. But even though the son was older, he had never married and had always lived at home. He was what we would call mentally challenged today; he was slow back then.

The elderly neighbor was brought back home for visitation, and friends and family came and went all afternoon and into the evening. After supper was over and the meal was cleared away and the dishes washed, the women gathered up the widow and took her to one of their homes to spend the night while the menfolk stayed up with the dead. The men chosen for this duty could be any mixture of relatives, close friends, church members, or anyone else who knew the deceased.

My grandfather was a deacon in the church where the family attended, so he was one of the ones who volunteered to stay the night, along with a small knot of other community members, at the side of the coffin of the dead man as the departed spent one last night in his bedroom before burial the next day.

After the grieving widow had left with the other women, the house grew still and quiet, the sitters not knowing what to say or even whether to say anything. For a long while, the only sounds heard were the ticking of the mantle clock, the crack of the fireplace, and the slow squeaks coming

---

OLD TIME CAMP MEETING PLACE. The spirit world and the Spirit world dominated life a hundred years ago. Even when farm families took vacation, it was to go to the campgrounds for a two-week long revival meeting. But don't you know they told the kids ghost stories after the evening service?

from the rocking chairs where the sitters were sitting and performing their duty of watching.

The slow son was one of the ones staying behind to sit up all night with his dad. All of a sudden one of the men spoke. And although he was talking in hushed tones, compared to the stillness and in the setting of the occasion, everyone jumped as if he were shouting. Which got them all tickled. Which loosened things up enough so that after a while, they decided to start telling jokes to stay awake.

At first, they just politely snickered at the punch lines out of respect for the dead man lying in front of them. But after a few hours, that wore off, and they were howling with laughter. They continued to top one another's stories all night.

As the sun started to rise, the women returned and the all-night sitters got up to go home. The son was still giggling as he followed the group of men out to the front porch. As they stood there, the boy slapped Granddaddy on the back and told them all he couldn't remember when he had had a better time. Then he added, "I just can't WAIT for Mama to die!"

Many years ago, Halloween fell on a Saturday night. Way back then, WLBT did not air *Saturday Night Live*, live. Management thought the show a little raw for Jackson, Mississippi, so it was tape delayed for a half-hour and aired almost live at 11:00 p.m. Usually, we filled the gap after the ten o'clock news ended and *Saturday Night Live* began with *Barney Miller* or *Andy Griffith* or something like that. Since I had already heard a bunch of ghost stories while doing *Look Around*

Mississippi, I asked the boss if he minded if I put together a half-hour of the ghost tales to run between 10:30 and 11:00 that Halloween night. His only question was, was it going to cost him anything? When he found out it wasn't, he was all for it.

NEIGHBORS. It would be from the pool of some of these folks that would come the people who would be expected to volunteer to sit up with the dead overnight.

SIGN OF HALLOWEEN. Jo and I took a wrong road at Michigan City, Mississippi (look it up on a map, way north). and had pulled into the driveway of a spooky old house to turn around and saw this sign. We didn't park.

So I got hold of Scott Kelly again, and we began trooping around the area going to haunted places and getting people to tell us their ghostly experiences. After we had collected six or seven good stories, we went out to the Haley Cemetery in an isolated, heavily wooded area near the Natchez Trace east of Madison to video the introductions to the stories there.

The Haley Cemetery was a very spooky place back then. It's about to be in the middle of a housing development now. But back then, you got there by taking a poorly paved road off Rice Road in Madison County and going under the Natchez Trace. Then the pavement turned to gravel. And the gravel turned into two ruts with knee-high Johnson grass growing between them on into the woods. Then you stopped the car and got out and took a narrow footpath on through the thickest part of the woods to the cemetery.

Dusk was almost settling in by the time we made it to the first gravestones. In the gathering darkness, we set lights and used the evaporating rays of the fast-setting sun filtering in orange and low through the dimming trees to create really eerie moods. Spider webs were shot with me standing beyond, out of focus as I recall, and things like that. I spoke low and matter-of-factly.

The only frightening thing that happened while we were there was we heard a four-wheeler zooming up the path where the car was parked. And we knew whoever was driving wouldn't be expecting a car to be stopped in the middle of his track. So we ran back toward the car yelling and waving to try to warn the driver before he wound up in the trunk with the rest of the camera equipment. It worked. When he saw two figures in the dim twilight running at him from the cemetery with arms flailing above their heads, he turned right around and left instantly!

So we edited the Haley Cemetery introductions in with the stories we had already produced and aired them that Halloween night. Scott and I enjoyed shooting the ghost stories so much that we decided we'd do a video of them to sell. Over the next year, we'd collect as many ghost stories as we could, release the collection just before Halloween, and get rich! Well, we got the stories and did the tape, but we're still waiting to get rich from it.

But a funny thing happened over the course of the year. Going all over and talking to people everywhere who are otherwise sane, having them tell me of their ghostly experiences in their houses or businesses or wherever, I evidently had unconsciously evolved into a ghost believer. I didn't realize it until nearly a year later when it came time to put together our ghost story tape and get it on the market.

FAIRY RING. Botanists would tell us mushrooms are fungi, and as they deplete their food source at their point of origin, they start to fan out and grow in a ring in search of more. Old superstition mentions more of magic and where witches dance at midnight.

USM ROSES. There's the old country song about give me my roses while I'm living. I'll take them both times, myself. But if you want to enjoy the most gorgeous roses in Mississippi, visit the All American Rose Garden on USM's campus in Hattiesburg.

OUTGROWN AND FORGOTTEN. The same way our playhouses fade and fall, so go our childhoods. That's why we try to believe in ghosts as adults. So maybe when we're finished having to be old, we can go and play again. Granddaughter Taylor and I had a contest to see who could get the best shot of the playhouse. This is her shot.

DELTA BOTTLE TREE. Most, if not all, of the bottle trees we see today are for decoration. But the old folks set them out in earnest, to trap inside the bottles the kinds of nuisance spirits that flit about and do things like hide stuff and waste money. We set up a bottle tree of our own, but evidently it was too far from the house to do any good.

Scott and I had already edited all the individual episodes, and all we needed were the introductions for the individual stories to tie the whole thing into a single unit. So we headed out for Haley Cemetery again late one afternoon.

But when we turned off Rice Road and onto the bad blacktop, even before we went under the Natchez Trace, a funny thing happened. The hair on the back of my neck started standing on end. I was actually scared to go all the way back into the deep dark woods to the old graveyard that last year at this time had been such a lark! I was surprised at myself for feeling so. But it was real fear! So I made up some kind of excuse, like the road was likely to have mudholes in it and we might get stuck. Maybe Scott was feeling the same thing because it didn't take much to convince him to turn around.

We ended up in a cemetery just one block off Main Street in downtown Madison. You could faintly see streetlights through the far tree line from where we were; we were so close to other people. Since I had to be back at work to do the 10:00 p.m. weather that night, we had to get busy quickly.

As Scott was setting up the camera, I pulled my car to the rear of the cemetery and put the headlights on bright and taped blue gels over them. Meanwhile, Scott had hung a couple of powerful battery lights in some small trees around a particular group of graves that would be our set.

On the way, we had stopped at a fireworks stand and bought it out of smoke bombs. We picked up a pan from Scott's barbeque grill to light them in so we wouldn't start a grass fire in the graveyard.

We found out pretty quickly that the smoke bombs only burned for about thirty seconds. So if we were going to use them for a fog effect, I'd have to spit my lines out with no flubs the first time. So we got set to shoot the first intro. Lights in place, camera rolling. Scott lit the smoke bomb and set it just out of camera view so the smoke would blow through the frame as I talked.

But the light breeze was erratic that night, and just as I started delivering my lines, the smoke drifted the other direction. Camera still rolling, Scott ran and grabbed the pan with the half-spent smoke bomb spewing away and dashed to the other side of me so we could save the line and the smoke. It seemed as if every time we tried to video an intro, the smoke would shift. So Scott was jumping all over the place that night.

A GREAT GULF DIVIDES. You wonder where those gone before are and what are they doing? You wish you could see them again until you go to a fog-shrouded graveyard. Then you don't want it to be right now.

GHOST TALES TOLD HERE. Screened porches in the summertime and fireplaces in the winter were two of the necessary ingredients for developing our fondness for storytelling. And if the late-night stories don't drift to tales of haunted houses, then you're not doing it right.

HAUNTED BRIDGE. There are just a few of these old iron relics left in the state. The way they creak and moan when you cross them gives you the willies. They way they creak and moan when no one is crossing them gives you the willie-ers!

NEWT KNIGHT WAS HERE and Major McLemore's blood stained the floor to prove it. A new floor now covers the stains. The porch door through which Knight entered and shot the Major still opens and slams on its own at times.

TAYLOR GROCERY. I've not heard any ghost stories about the store but plenty of tales about liquid spirits flowing all hours of the night and early mornings in the days when Willie Morris held court here while writer-in-residence just up the road at Ole Miss.

TUTWILER MURAL. The panel depicting Sonny Boy Williams on the wall of murals celebrating Tutwiler as the place where W. C. Handy first heard the blues gives me the creeps just looking at it. I've not had the time to actually follow the map to the grave.

It was a quiet street. Only one car came along the entire time we were in there doing our taping, and it didn't go all the way past us. Matter of fact, it rounded a little curve just before the cemetery and locked its brakes and slid slightly sideways in the road before going in reverse and quickly turning around and leaving. I was wondering what was wrong with that guy. Then I looked back around at the cemetery, luminous in the soft blue of my headlights and the spent smoke hanging in threads low to the ground with graves glowing, and a couple of guys jumping tombs with a dish of smoking incense. I'm sure the driver must have thought some sort of devil worshiping or something was going on.

But that's how I came to respect the notion of the existence of ghosts, just taking a year and going around the state and talking to people and them telling me what all had happened to them in a supernatural way. It points out the truth of what the Bible says about faith comes by hearing. You hear enough about anything and you'll start to believe it. It happened that way with me and Scott and ghosts!

DUSK DARK AND FOGGY were the conditions when a propane truck driver got directions from a lady who'd been dead for twenty years. I've asked people alive right now for directions who didn't have a clue. Maybe I should come back later.

GOLD HOLE ROAD. The sign north of Roxie is about all you can see of the Gold Hole today. The actual lake is on private property and is so overgrown you can't even tell where it is anymore.

I'm sitting here, gazing out the window thinking about all the other ghost tales I have heard over the years, most of them firsthand accounts. For instance, a fellow told me that one January he and his family were caught by surprise when a sudden deep cold snap hit. He said they lived in a house trailer way back off some obscure road that turned off Redbone Road in Warren County. They had run out of propane, and they had a little baby, and all of them were getting pretty cold. They had called in an order to the gas company, and the driver had them on his list. However, it was getting late, and this particular driver had never delivered to them before and was a little fuzzy about how to get way back off the main road to their trailer. The fellow telling me the story said he was kind of surprised when the gas truck showed up in his yard because usually when someone came there for the first time, they'd have to call for directions or he'd have to go meet them somewhere and let them follow him in.

The driver explained he didn't have a bit of trouble in the world after he stopped at a little rundown house on a corner of Redbone Road and asked the old lady sitting there if she knew where such and such family lived. She directed the driver right to them.

The man telling me the story said he was a little baffled when the driver again told him exactly which house he had stopped at and what the old lady looked like. The driver said she was tiny and stooped over, wearing a bonnet and smoking a pipe. The man let out a "whew" and, shaking his head, told the driver that the lady he had described sounded exactly like his great-grandmother who had lived in that house until she died twenty years earlier, and no one had lived in that house since then.

I've seen the house, and sure enough, there are never any lights on and no one is ever around, and you can tell the place has been deserted a long time. And I bet after the story of the gas delivery got out, they were never bothered with trespassers.

Spirits are supposed to guard treasure, too. I didn't know if you knew that or not. But savvy treasure hunters use this to their advantage with all sorts of devices that tune in to the spirit world, revealing what the spirits are guarding.

The best story about using some kind of device to find buried treasure is associated with the Gold Hole near Roxie. Natchez Trace robbers were supposed to have used this particular spot in Franklin County to bury their loot in an iron pot with a heavy lid on it. For some reason, either they died or were arrested or something, but they never came back for the buried treasure. People knew it existed, but they didn't know exactly where it was.

Scott Kelly and I used the Roxie Gold Hole as one of the stories on another venture we never completed, a video about buried treasure in Mississippi. We were shooting the story when we went to Roxie and talked to Mr. Whitehead, a former mayor of the town. He knew all about the bandits

and the rumors and the search for the gold over the decades, and he told us what he knew.

He started his story back years and years before, when a couple of fellows came to the owner of the land where the treasure was supposed to have been hidden and told her they had a device that would locate the buried pot of gold. And to prove it would work, they handed the lady a gold coin and told her to hide it somewhere in the house; they would then find it with their device. She agreed that if they could find the hidden gold coin then she would allow them to look for the buried treasure on her land.

So she slipped from the front porch back through the living room and kitchen to a bedroom off the kitchen at the back of the house and slipped the gold coin into a top bureau drawer. Then she came back to the front porch and told the men she was ready. They pulled out their device. But to everyone's surprise, the machine didn't point toward the direction the woman had gone. It pointed to another bedroom just off the porch. The lady followed the men as they followed their arrow into that bedroom. The machine pointed to a chest of drawers and then to the middle drawer. The lady opened the drawer and discovered a gold coin in it that had evidently been lost and forgotten about.

Convinced, she let the men begin looking. It didn't take long before they had a hit. Out came the shovels, and the gold hole was started. Three or four feet under the surface they struck something solid. An iron pot! But before they could clear all the dirt off the lid and open it, it started to rain. And you know how hard one of our afternoon thunderstorms can get in no time at all. Soon, the shallow hole the men had dug was full of water. It was late in the day already, so the treasure hunters decided to get out of the rain and come back in the morning and get a fresh, dry start to finish raising their prize.

The land around Roxie is loess soil. Geologists say loess could be described as rock-flour. Boulders out west were ground into dust by prehistoric glaciers, they say. And as the ice started melting, the ground-up rocks were sifted and picked up by the prevailing westerly winds and carried hundreds and hundreds of miles and deposited here where the prevailing westerlies quit prevailing, on the east bank of the Mississippi River and then on past for some thirty or so miles.

GOLD HOLE. This is a still frame of video from the day Mr. Whitehead, Scott Kelly, and I visited the Gold Hole. It looks like any other farm pond that's been allowed to grow up. Scott manned the camera that day.

GOLD HOLE CABLE. The stuff that dreams are made of is supposed to be attached to the other end of this cable taut from where it has grown into the trunk of a pine tree on one end, hooked to something at the bottom of the Gold Hole on the other. Video still frame shot by Scott Kelly. Our Gold Hole adventure ended when we found the cable.

MR. WHITEHEAD AND THE CABLE. There were old photographs of Mr. Whitehead holding this same cable in the day when there were no trees and underbrush hiding the Gold Hole. It was like finding something you've forgotten you've lost the day we stumbled upon it.

One characteristic of loess soil is that when it gets wet, it takes on the consistency of molasses. So when the treasure hunters returned to their hole the next morning, the iron pot had disappeared, sunk under the murk and mud, and was out of sight again. So they dug out the muck until they struck something hard and metallic once more. Only the pot kept slipping away in the saturated ooze collected at the bottom of the hole. All day, every time they hit the pot, it would just sink deeper and deeper into the quicksand-like earth surrounding it.

Long story short, this hitting and pushing away went on for years. Shovels were replaced by a steam shovel after a while. And more than one steam shovel was used before too long. The hole grew larger and deeper and flooded with every rain, and pumping equipment was brought in, and the hole dried out and was dug deeper. A barge was floated on the surface of the pond that formed after it got so deep it could no longer be pumped out, and a dragline was put on the barge, and the hole went deeper and deeper and wider.

Mr. Whitehead said it was high entertainment for decades around Roxie to watch them dig for the pot of gold. He said someone had the presence of mind to wrap a wire cable like the ones used on dragline buckets to the handle of the iron pot one time when the pot was close enough to the surface to feel it. And they tied the other end of the cable around a pine tree way up on the bank of the pond that the gold hole had become by then.

Then, sometime in the 1960s, suddenly, overnight, all activity stopped at the Gold Hole. One morning, the equipment was gone and the treasure hunters were gone. Left there was only silence and the sizable lake created over the decades by the digging of the treasure hunters. Some say it's a hundred feet deep. The day Scott and Mr. Whitehead and I walked around it, it seemed to be at least five hundred feet wide.

Tramping the upper lip of the bank of the Gold Hole wasn't easy. It was overgrown in briars and huckleberry bushes and thirty-year-old pines. We were trying to get a good vantage point from which to shoot some video of the pond to show how big it really was. Scott was manning the camera that day. I was following Mr. Whitehead. We maneuvered as close to the water as we could, where we could, which wasn't very close because the pond didn't have very much of a beach. Its banks were all pretty sheer, on average over ten feet high, straight down.

As we were trying to get to one place that looked promising, blocking our progress was a heavy wire cable, grown into a pine tree trunk on one end and stretched taut and attached to something under the water in the Gold Hole on the other. The sight of the cable took Mr. Whitehead's breath away. This was it! The fabled cable that was supposed to be anchored to the pot.

Was it? Did the other end of it actually hook to what had been the goal of countless treasure hunters for over half a century? Or was it simply attached to the sunken barge, as someone else told me. Whichever. It was proof that something had gone on here.

Was there really ever any gold in the bottom of the Gold Hole? Who knows? I don't. But there were dreams dreamed and acted upon here beyond the shadow of a doubt. That's the spirit of the Gold Hole. That somebody believed in something enough to actually do something in pursuit of it. The very existence of the hole itself proves that.

We wanted to do some more exploring with the camera that afternoon, but it started to rain, so we quit and went back home.

I'm No Daniel Boone

I AM NOT AN OUTDOORSMAN. I have friends who are and invite me to sleep under the stars with them all the time. Kirk and Rita Hill in Mendenhall come to mind readily. Kirk was the last person to talk me into coming along on a campout several years ago. It had been so long since I had used my sleeping bag that I had forgotten the zipper was broken. The only place it would clasp was right there where the zipper device was. It opened out either side.

It was November. (Why do people go camping in November, anyway?) A cold rain had fallen all day, followed by clearing and wind that night. After storytelling around the campfire finally wound down, I climbed into the tent and discovered the malfunction in my sleeping bag. It's hard to wrap up snugly in a sleeping bag when the zipper doesn't work.

About the time I would get my feet covered, my top would come loose. Then when I fixed the top, somehow my feet would pop out. I sleeplessly fought that thing for hours. Finally after great intensity and effort, I was snug head to toe. And about then I had to get up and go use the bathroom. I gave up and swore off camping out.

That's why I resisted so strongly when *Mississippi Roads* wanted me to do a story about Biloxi's Ohr Museum's artist retreat on Horn Island. It was a campout. The artists who signed up stayed in tents for a week and took courses and created and generally got away from soccer games and cell phones to give their minds a break so they could think and create again.

The premise of the outing was wonderful; a sabbatical on a deserted island so soul and spirit could get acquainted again while pursuing creativity with like-minded peers. It was the application of it that didn't appeal to me: camping out. My idea of roughing it is when the air-conditioner makes a noise in my motel room, or I have to watch black and white television.

Fortunately, for years I had an automatic excuse for not having to go on the artist retreat. It was always held in May, and May is a ratings month. Since I was doing weather at WLBT at the

---

RAINBOW. A rainbow may just be the physics of refracted light, but it always lifts my spirits. And you'll always see people pointing one out. That's why I liked weather on TV. It was important to everybody.

time, I couldn't take a night off during ratings, so therefore I couldn't go to Horn Island overnight to do the story. And since I knew I had an ironclad excuse, I could feign disappointment when I'd get my annual reminder from the folks at Ohr. I could go on and on about how wonderful it would be to go with them but still be able to regretfully decline because I couldn't take off during ratings.

One day that changed. Had I remembered that if freed from weather I'd be obliged to go camping on Horn Island I might have given the boss a different answer.

What happened was, one day my boss, Dan Modisett at WLBT, took me to lunch and revealed a bit of audience research the station had just conducted. It seems they were getting a lot of voluntary mentions of my stories, *Look Around Mississippi*, when that wasn't even what they were researching at all. So they figured if the people they were interviewing associated *Look Around* with WLBT so much, maybe we should be giving them a bit more of it.

So Dan told me it was my decision, but would I like to give up weather and do *Look Around* stories full-time from now on. I told him to let me think about it and then said, "Okay," all in the same sentence.

Way back yonder, *Look Around Mississippi* originally came into my life when it became apparent that Woodie Assaf wasn't going to retire from being WLBT's full-time weather anchor nearly as soon as anyone expected. I had been hired to be Woodie's replacement upon the eventuality of his retirement. But until he decided to go, I'd do feature stories and just the 10:00 p.m. weathercast. I spent over fifteen wonderful years of my life doing just that. I could go anywhere I wanted during the day and bring back any story I wanted just so long as I got back in time to do the ten o'clock weather.

Then one day it happened. Woodie retired. Suddenly, I had to be in the office every afternoon on time and to stay there until eleven o'clock every night. I was getting cabin fever from being confined to the weather set all day, every day. It really took only about two weeks for me to realize

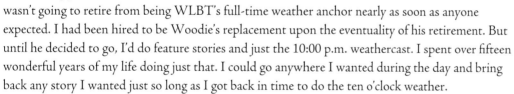

KIRK HILL DRIVING, ME WALKING. Evidently, my friend Kirk Hill is off on another adventure. If it entails camping out, then he can email me photos of it later.

THE ROCKY SPRINGS CHURCH meets every Sunday and is attended by many campers from the campground nearby just off the Natchez Trace. I repented of camping the morning after.

SIGNS IN THE SKY have always intrigued me. They warn of what's coming if you know how to read them.

that after waiting in the wings for all those years for this moment, it was too late. I had fallen more in love with doing *Look Around Mississippi*.

I loved doing the weather, too. Don't get me wrong. I got that from Daddy. In his business, he traveled the roads of the Delta every day and had work crews outside every day, so weather was very important to him. On the cable in Greenville, he could get Bob Neblett on WJTV at the beginning of the newscast, then whoever was on Channel 7 out of Little Rock doing weather in the middle, then tune in Woodie on WLBT at the end. Then Daddy added up what they all said and divided by three and came up with what he thought was really going to happen.

Daddy would have loved The Weather Channel, but he passed away before it ever came on. However, my sister Ermie and her husband, Hank, in North Carolina swore Daddy's spirit must have visited their house for a while. Because every night at 9:00 p.m., their television set would come on by itself, and it would be tuned to The Weather Channel. They still call it the Frank Grayson Memorial Channel.

RIVER AND CLOUDS, NATCHEZ. Weather, nature, and the city of Natchez—three of my favorite things in one shot.

HORN ISLAND. Any vestige of civilization you may need on Horn Island, make sure you pack it along with you. And don't leave it behind when you leave.

PASCAGOULA RIVER AND MOONRISE. It's as magic a river as any on earth. It sings if you have ears to hear it. The Pascagoula widens into the Gulf with Horn Island twelve miles to the south.

HORN ISLAND DUNES. Each dune and each ravine in between had a name. I hope they're still there after Katrina.

Here's another aside on the Spirit of Frank Grayson. My other sister, Linda, and her husband, Jim, had sort of an unsettling, but comforting, experience themselves. Daddy loved to play Rook. (For a Baptist, he was a pretty good card player.) Years after Daddy passed away, on the evening of his birthday, a deck of Rook cards leapt off Jim and Linda's coffee table and onto the floor at about the same hour Hank and Ermie's TV tuned in The Weather Channel. Was that Daddy? Come on. Would we have liked for it to be? Oh my gosh, yes! So I could ask him all those questions I never thought to ask him while he was here but only came to mind after he was gone.

But back in Greenville, I'd watch all those weathercasts along with Daddy and grew quite fond of the idea of one day being a TV weatherman myself. And who knew back then that I'd not only get to do so but also get to work with my hero, Woodie, for all those years?

But also through all those years waiting out the main weather anchor slot, I was getting to see a lot of the state and getting to tell a lot of stories. And once Woodie retired, I frankly missed the travel and the freedom.

Also, I realized we had lots of other folks at the station who trained to do nothing but weather, and they would probably like for me to move on out of the main spot and not hang around so they could get their careers together a lot sooner than I had been able to. But we had no one else who had any inclination to do anything like *Look Around Mississippi*. And here we had our researchers saying the public was bringing up the subject on their own and asking for *Look Around* by name.

So when Dan asked if I was at all interested in dropping weather and doing *Look Around*, it didn't take much of a sales pitch for me to heartily agree to do so.

Now, in all fairness, I will admit I missed doing the weather for a long time after leaving it behind. After all, for over fifteen years, through lots of life changes including a divorce, the 10:00 p.m. weather was the only secure factor I had at times. And when I gave up the weather position, it wasn't exactly as if my life had settled down by then. To a great degree, it was even more up in the air than

PINES, HORN ISLAND. Having to stand in against the constant winds and salt spray molds the pines into shapes we're not used to inland.

NIGHTFALL AT HORN ISLAND drops shadows of twilight over tent city. But wait a little and the merriment starts at the bonfire.

YARD ART. The kinds of things that can decorate any yard.

COLD SNAP. Weather like this could freeze Daddy in his tracks. That's why he kept up with it and I got interested in it.

it had ever been. And the one area of stability I had always counted on I was allowing to be passed on to someone else.

For several years off and on, I have helped Michael Rubenstein prepare the video clips that go on the kiosks at the Mississippi Sports Hall of Fame and Museum of the inductees into the Hall of Fame for that year. I remember one former NFL player who had been traded to the Saints late in his career. (His take on it was when he went to the Saints, it wasn't like the team had had twenty years of experience. They had one year's experience twenty times.) After a season or two, in a disagreement with the front office, he suddenly retired from football.

His reaction was similar to mine at giving up weather. He said he felt like he was in freefall without a parachute. Football was all he knew. Now it was gone.

That was me. The last stable rug in my life had been pulled from under me and I was in freefall. And nobody knew. And I couldn't tell anybody lest they began to think it was because I didn't like *Look Around*. Mama would have told me that in times like these, depend on Jesus. And probably I did a lot more than I realize. And still do.

But what jarred me out of that post-weather funk hit me like a bolt from the blue. All of a sudden, a change in perspective swept over me during the 10:00 p.m. newscast one night. I was lying upstairs in my bed in my underwear watching TV when it struck me suddenly, "What am I thinking? Why would I want to still be downtown in a coat and tie like all those other folks at this time of night when I can be right here comfortable at home with the family?"

The greatest advantage of being free of daily weather chores was that I could now do full-time the job that before I had had to squeeze in around my weather schedule. I could conceive of no disadvantages until the next May and the phone rang.

It was Key Ivy, the producer of *Mississippi Roads*, telling me the Ohr people are so excited I can go along to Horn Island with them this year since I no longer have to stay home because of weather during the May ratings, and especially since I had sounded so disappointed in years past when I explained why I couldn't go.

Horn Island has been an artist's retreat for years, Walter Anderson being the most famous artist to have sojourned there. Anderson's weeks-long stays on Horn are legendary among the collectors of his pottery decorations and block prints and watercolors. He would row the twelve miles from Ocean Springs to Horn and beyond to the Chandeleur Islands, where he sketched the plants and animals and discovered to his satisfaction the relationship between mankind and nature.

The George Ohr Museum picked Horn Island for their artists' retreats not because Walter

RED AT NIGHT glints through the top of an ancient cypress in a swamp out from Belzoni. You can't be in a weather studio in Jackson and get to see the sunset in a Delta swamp. I chose the swamps.

Anderson had been there, but for many of the same reasons he chose to go there: isolation and abundant subject matter.

But there are no modern conveniences on Horn Island that you don't bring along with you. Nothing. Just sand, plants, and animals. And mosquitoes. The mosquitoes are so abundant they form a category all to themselves. So to stay there for a week means tents and sleeping bags and insect repellent and not even black-and-white TV.

Next thing I knew, Jo and I were looking for the dock in Ocean Springs from which the daily iceboat launched. We were loaded down with camping equipment we had borrowed from Bert Case, who is an avid overnighter on the Pearl River back home.

I was looking for a big boat since we were going out twelve miles across the Mississippi Sound into open water. What I found was the kind of open-air job that I see on the reservoir a lot but wouldn't have thought of taking out into the Gulf. Especially with it loaded down with the daily ration of ice, and camping equipment belonging to Jo and me and a couple of newspaper reporters along for the overnight trip, as well as camera gear and all us people.

The wind had been out of the southeast for several days before our excursion, so we had a headwind and a pretty good chop to contend with on the way out. Our youthful driver was of the age that he could not die. I don't think he realized he had passengers who could.

He was standing at the wheel of the boat when we rounded the last bit of reeds and headed into

HORN ISLAND MORNING. Clouds and distant rain showers further mute the soft light of dawn. I was checking to make sure our boat home was still there.

HORN ISLAND ISOLATION. On most days, the rest of the world does little more than float past Horn Island. If you want to be alone, you can have all you want of it here.

the open water. As soon as everything was clear, he opened her up full throttle. At first it was okay, until we started hitting the chop. We would go airborne off the top of a wave and BLAM, bottom out on the next. Then we'd sail up again and bottom out again. Our driver was standing, so his knees could buckle and absorb the shock that the rest of us were taking directly up our backbones seated. After a few landings, I turned to Jo and told her I thought my spine was compressing. I didn't think my shirt would fit any longer by the time we got to the island. Jo was in tears.

I tugged at our driver's shirttail and told him that, geologically speaking, it was generally accepted that Horn Island had been there for a million years or so, and I was sure it would still be there even if we slowed down a bit.

The first order of business after we landed and shook hands with our hosts was to find a place to pitch the tent. They told us that if we set it up on sea oats we would be arrested. I thought I knew what sea oats looked like, but to be safe, we selected a spot right in the middle of tent city. I figured if I did something wrong there, they'd have to take us all in.

After putting up the tent, we asked where the bathroom was. Directions sent us down a path, over a sand dune to a lagoon, then turn left and look behind a big clump of live oak shrubs. There we would find a potty seat on four legs and a shovel. Bring your own paper. And just as you went over the top of the sand dune, there was a post with a red flag on it. When you went to the facility, you took the red flag with you. That way, if you came to the post and the red flag was gone, you'd know someone was in there already.

After that, Jo and I set about for the afternoon's work. I documented the artists' classes and what they were creating while she was already packing for home. Another thing I wanted to do was to get as much video footage of Horn Island as I could while I was there, the idea being that next time I wanted to do a story about the island, I could just reach for my file footage and not have to go back out.

I hung mostly on the north shore of the island where the dunes drop off abruptly to a narrow beach with the water of the Mississippi Sound lapping on the sands. Then I got carried away with the plant life on the island. All those pine trees in the Walter Anderson watercolors really look like that. I thought he was making caricatures when he drew trees with limbs turned as if they were ladies just coming out of the beauty parlor poufing their hair.

I climbed to the top of the dune and got shots of the artists' tent city down below and the Gulf of Mexico a mile away on the other side of the island. Then I wandered down the other side of the sand dune to a lagoon ringed with pines. About that time, a lady came walking briskly over the top of the dune carrying the red flag. As she abruptly stopped, I realized this was the loo lagoon. I was on the path between her and the facility. Embarrassed, I started to fold my tripod and apologized and told her I'd leave. She replied, "No time. Just look the other way."

So I whipped my camera back around the little blue lake at my back and spied an osprey nest

---

THE LOO LAGOON. Hang a left and look for the clump of live oaks. And bring your own paper.

HORN ISLAND GROUND COVER. It isn't sea oats. But I'd still not pitch a tent on it.

NORTH SHORE, HORN ISLAND. I've not been back to Horn Island since Katrina. But I understand the storm surge considerably resculpted the sandy features of the island.

LOOK THE OTHER WAY and discover an osprey nest at the other end of the lagoon.

in a tall pine at the other end and zoomed in on that for a few minutes.

Shortly, the lady came back, much more relaxed now. She said, "You know, it's awfully disconcerting using the bathroom like this." I told her I guess so, with some guy with a camera down here. She answered, "No, it's not that. It's just that the wind blows where it's never blown before!"

The rain that must accompany any outing like this came and ran along the sand under the tent. Anything on the air mattress survived. Everything else was gritty. Supper was gritty that night in response to the continued brisk southeast wind. The wind did keep the bugs away, however—that was good.

During the night, sleep was impossible. I'm used to a flat bed. This one had a decided downhill list. And the air mattress kept deflating. One minute you're as comfortable as the conditions would allow. The next you're flat on the sand again.

Along about 3:00 or 4:00 a.m., I discovered the problem with putting our tent right in the middle of everyone else's. Jo and I both had to go to the bathroom. And in the middle of tent city, there was no way to just step outside. No, we had to follow the path over the sand dune to the lagoon.

I don't know what got us so tickled. Probably it was because I told Jo to be quiet. Then she giggled even louder, and then I caught it. Then tent lights were coming on all around us, so we hurried away in the darkness.

But the sun also rises. And finally it did. We had the tent down and packed away. All the cameras were in big Ziploc bags away from the sand. And we would be ready for the return ride to the mainland after we made one last trip over the sand dune.

Being a gentleman, I let Jo go first. As she sat down, she let out a scream. I thought the potty lid was cold or something. But I looked where she was pointing out into the lagoon, and there was an eight-foot alligator about ten feet off shore. He was looking at us about the way I look over the menu at IHOP. It didn't take Jo but about forty-five seconds to finish, and we were out of there.

SQUATTERS RIGHTS. On Horn, the ospreys own the place. Don't get near their nests. And don't step on sea oats. And don't leave any trash behind when you leave. And be careful where you step—snakes. And don't swim in the lagoon—alligators. Let's don't even talk about the bugs. But have a good time and come back soon.

EIGHT-FOOTER. Actually, this isn't the alligator we saw at the lagoon the morning we were leaving. There was little time for photo ops that day. This one was floating in the lake at the Noxubee Wildlife Refuge in north Mississippi. But if you've run from one, you've run from them all.

TISHOMINGO CABIN. They're not big at all. But they're big enough to get lost from everyday life in, for a weekend or a week, while you wish it could be longer.

On the way back to the tent, I reflected on that experience. I told Jo I thought I'd get an alligator for our bathroom back home because she'd never managed to get ready to go anywhere this fast before.

I haven't been back to Horn Island since Hurricane Katrina. I've heard that the storm surge did major damage to the pines and the sand dunes and the wildlife. As much as I pretend I didn't like it, I loved Horn Island. True, I wouldn't have wanted to spend weeks on end there as Walter Anderson did.

As part of the Gulf Islands National Seashore managed by the National Park Service, Horn Island is kept in as natural a state as possible. When we were there, it was about as close to the way the barrier islands were before the Europeans came as it had been in decades. Now that the huge natural force known as Katrina has rearranged even what we saw, Horn must be as close to being "untouched" as ever in recorded history.

Although I don't care for roughing-it type camping, I do like the rustic CCC cabins we have at some of the state parks in Mississippi, Tishomingo State Park in particular. That's where Jo taught me to cuss.

We were going to shoot three episodes of *Mississippi Roads* in northeast Mississippi on a Wednesday, Thursday, and Friday of one week. So I thought I'd go ahead and just take vacation for the whole week from WLBT, and we'd get a cabin at Tishomingo State Park for that Monday through Thursday night. By the way, weeknights are fairly open at state parks; weekends stay booked up for weeks in advance. But if you want to just run away for a couple of nights on the spur of the moment, call a state park and get a cabin.

The cabins have the feel of old settlers' places to them. They are not made of logs, but you'd think they were. Knotty cypress. Big native stone fireplaces. Wrap-around screened-in porches with picnic tables and swings hanging on chains from the ceiling beams.

As an added bonus, Bear Creek was just below our cabin. That Monday after Jo and I unpacked, we had a little time for exploring, so we hit the rock outcroppings across the swinging bridge that spans Bear Creek. Had I grown up here, we'd have played hide-and-seek and army in the rocks.

Although there is a fish and steak house where the driveway to the park turns off Highway 25, they're only open on the weekends. So I fixed a breakfast-type supper of bacon, eggs, and biscuits in the little kitchen at the cabin. The aroma of the frying bacon fit right in with the leftover smells of the fires in the fireplace and reminded me of what Grandmother's house smelled like back when she was still living and cooked breakfast on her old wood burning stove.

Later, we sat together and rocked slowly in the porch swing and listened to the night, adding the slow rhythm of our squeaking swing chains to it. It was great. No television, no telephone, just Bear Creek gurgling down below and the crickets.

The next day, we zipped down to Fulton and visited Aunt Coleen, still living in Grandmother's house, and then hit the flea markets along Highway 25. That night, we again sat in the stillness of the evening. No television, no telephone, just Bear Creek and the crickets.

BEAR CREEK IN THE MIST. The creek flows north. That's a little different for our part of the country. But it fits right in with Tishomingo Park, which is also different from typical Mississippi topography.

TISHOMINGO HIDDEN SPOT. You go to Tishomingo to lose yourself and end up finding simple treasures like this waterfall stream.

COTTON PLANT is the type of little town you'll discover in an afternoon's driving distance of Tishomingo Park.

The next day, the crew was there, and we shot the first of our three episodes of *Mississippi Roads* in Corinth. When we finished, the crew from ETV went to their motel rooms and Jo and I skipped back down to our quiet little cabin at Tishomingo State Park. No telephone, no television, just the swing and the creek and the crickets.

However, the peace and quiet was overwhelming after a while, I guess, because suddenly Jo jumped up and said, "If I hear one more damn cricket, I'm going to step on him!"

These are the good old days. If we could only realize that fact while we are living them. Then when we grow older and tell stories about these days, the memories of them will be all the sweeter.

CHUNKY RIVER, SEPTEMBER. You don't have to go twelve miles into the Gulf to get off by yourself. Places like these are quiet sabbaticals for your mind for a little or as long a time as you have to stay.

LAGOON AND GULF. You can see across Horn Island easily. Walking it through nothing but sand is a little tougher.

ROUGHING IT. Even the natural elements of Horn Island look like they have a hard time existing in the extremes of heat and cold and wet and dry there.

Mississippi Seasons

I WAS TALKING TO A LADY ONE TIME whose job it was to drive a delivery route along a certain stretch of roadway between a couple of towns in Mississippi. I made the comment to her that running up and down the same stretch of highway all the time must really get boring. She seemed surprised that I would think so. She explained that it was never really the same stretch of road twice, anyway. For instance, it was entirely different on sunny days than on rainy ones. And the changing of the seasons brought out even more of the personality of the roadway.

I thought maybe she was just saying that to convince herself. But then again, if you really notice, no two days are exactly alike, are they? Seasonal differences are the most drastic changes. Pick one spot. Then only come view it on just four days out of the year: one day in April, a day in August, another in October, and another in February. Even though it is the same place, all those seasonal differences would probably make it look like four different ones. Like us at ages 16, 30, 42, and 55—four different people, yet all the same person. But the day-to-day difference is almost imperceptible. Over time, you know the clock hands move, even if you can't perceive it while it's happening.

The physical changing of the seasons has little relation to the calendar in Mississippi. For instance, we've usually not had the first hint of fall-feeling weather until well after the official day for its arrival, September 21 or so. And if we had to wait as late as the celestial spring equinox for buds to start popping, we'd all die of winteritis. And winter's intensity comes and goes with the decades. Some of the early explorers described our area as being a place that knew no ice or snow. Then, on the other hand, another group of European explorers roaming around one winter in the pre-colonial period got caught in a blizzard in Mississippi and had to be aided by the Native Americans lest they froze to death. Subtropical parakeets used to live here—but so did the Ice Age mastodon.

Spring and winter have a tug of war some years. This spring, for example, dogwoods have already bloomed out and so have azaleas, almost. But we're expecting a late freeze tonight (April).

FALL ALONG THE FENCE. Scenes like this make a ride along the Trace enjoyable.

Back in the early 1800s when St. John's Episcopal Church on Lake Washington in the Delta was dedicated, the ceremony was cut short because of a freak snowstorm in mid-April. I never believed that could happen until this year as I sit finishing up details of this chapter on April 7, snug and warm beside the computer while the afternoon temperatures are dropping through the forties outside my Rankin County home. Hopefully, this will be the last blast of winter this season.

But most years, winter isn't so much a defined season here in Mississippi with a clear-cut beginning and a clear-cut ending as it is a few periods of cold snaps with warm-ups in between. Now, the cold can get very cold. I have seen the Barnett Reservoir frozen over. The wintering geese and ducks were really confused trying to find open water in which to set down. And some rare years those cold snaps can last more than a week, sometimes longer, before a letup. But then there are those years that I have had to run the car air-conditioner at least a day or so every month of the winter.

Summer in Mississippi is more a way of life than a season. Not taking anything away from the Beach Boys and their California surfing albums of the 1960s, but Mississippi could well be the land of endless summer, with 90-degree days starting in May and then holding out until after State Fair is over in October. Then, considering it takes a couple of months either side of the 90-degree days to warm up to them and, then later, to cool down from them, you can understand why I have more short-sleeved than long-sleeved shirts in my closet.

Summer is a noisy time. Constant chatter at the swimming pool or swimming hole, tractors zipping back and forth across fields, Little League until the Fourth of July. Nature joins in, too, with katydids calling to one another in the trees after dark. In early summer, we have a mockingbird that sings in her nest until after midnight in the cedars by the mailbox out by the street.

QUEEN ANNE'S CROWN. This is an "I'm a lucky dog" shot. I pulled over to the side of the road to shoot something else altogether when I saw the butterfly. This is summer.

HANG AROUND A WHILE. In Mississippi, on rare winter mornings when it's below freezing, about all water can do is wait until about noon to continue on its way.

DELTA WINTER FIELD. This is more the un-color of winter I remember from growing up in the Delta. Spring was always a treat after a monochrome season of grays, blacks, and whites.

DUCKS AND HARD WATER. It is a rarity for it to get cold enough here to freeze a pond, much less a lake. So rare in fact that ducks don't know what to make of it any more than we do.

THE STATE FAIR UNFURLS early October every year in Jackson. When it does, it's only a domino tumble or two until Christmas. Be ready.

CHRISTMAS PARADE, NATCHEZ. Strictly speaking, Christmas parades are fall events. And late November and early December can give conditions ranging from summer-like to chilly winter on any given day.

MY HOUSE IN SNOW. Do folks in Minnesota take pictures of their houses every time it snows? Of the twenty years I've had the barn, this is the only picture I can find with it covered in snow. I may not have had a camera handy the other time.

TRACKS IN THE SNOW. I snapped this in Flowood on my way to the TV station. I'd have rather had more time for picture taking that day.

SYRUP MAKING is making a comeback in Mississippi. More and more, the skilled master syrup cookers are passing their knowledge along to youngsters. And the youngsters want to learn how to keep the craft alive. Not only is it a throwback to simpler times, it tastes good!

When I was a boy, we played outdoors during the summer. So added to all the other noises were the sounds of a neighborhood baseball game with just as many umpires as there were players and the whirring of bicycles as we caravanned on two wheels all over Greenville—to the Paramount for the Thursday morning kids' feature, to the bar-pits behind the levee for fishing or playing army, and to school later in the fall.

The colors of summer are green, white, and blue: trees, clouds, and sky. Early summer, all of the trees are individuals, each with its own particular shade of green. Later in the summer, they all darken together and merge into a single mass of dark summer olive.

Every breath in summer is full of smells: new-mown grass or fresh spaded earth from someone's garden or flowerbed, and the sweet scent of honeysuckles tempting you to come gather a handful and then work for that one droplet of nectar hidden deep in the throat of each. Keri one time tried to get a jar-full of honeysuckle nectar. She worked for a few hours and didn't even get the bottom of the jar wet. However, I really think she ate most of the profit.

One of my favorite summer smells comes just before an afternoon cloudburst, the tang of rain that washes out ahead of the storm. It is a mixture of wet vegetation and wet earth, sometimes wet asphalt, that warns a shower is about to hit. Maybe there are electrical ions that come along with it from high up in the clouds because I always get a rush when I smell the rain on the way.

I don't want this to be a book about old times and long-ago places, necessarily. But since Mr. Faulkner has already established that in the South the past is never forgotten, it isn't even past (overlooking my disputing this still being applicable in my chapter on the Civil War), I won't

---

JO'S SNAP DRAGONS add more to our yard than color to the obligatory greens of summer.

LEAVES AND RAINDROPS are a part of the fragrance of an approaching shower. God did a good job when he made it smell before a rain.

I became a senior in high school that I had observed enough winters-into-springs that I started watching for the first signs of the changing of the seasons. In the Delta, those signs are a very

welcome sight because it means that color is coming back into what has otherwise been a black-and-white world over the winter months: gray sky, black buckshot dirt, and dead trees. My friend, Dave Dunaway, who was our head football coach and assistant principal at E. E. Bass Junior High in Greenville, told me about rabbit hunting in the Delta. Walking across plowed fields on a hunt, thick buckshot mud would stick to your boots until you were about eight feet tall.

Speaking of Coach Dunaway reminds me that our junior high football team was named "The Yannigans." Coach told me that one day early on in his career at Bass, he asked Mr. Solomon, the principal, what a yannigan was. In true educator fashion, Mr. Solomon told Coach Dunaway to go look it up. I asked Dave if he had, and he said he did. So I asked him what it meant. He told me to go look it up.

Winter into spring is the most abrupt change in seasons we have. Bulb flowers start blooming even while it is still cold. Then one day you notice the trees have a haze of green about them. Redbuds paint the roadsides and deep woods with purple splotches. And dogwood and azalea put in their two weeks. By that time, the weather has warmed up nicely.

Azalea fades into the crape myrtle and mimosa of summer. Warm days ease up to hot days. The deep greens of summer once again rob the trees of their individual lighter spring shades, and before you know it, it's all started again. Season after season blending life from page to page and year to year. And you don't notice it so much when it's happening, like trying to watch the hands of the clock move. It's only when you pause later and look back that you are aware that it isn't the same anymore.

DELTA WINTER COLOR. Don't let me or anyone else tell you there is never color in the Delta in winter. Who are you going to believe? Me, or your own eyes?

IT ALWAYS HAPPENS. Spring always comes. Usually, just when you can't stand another bleak day.

The Last Mile

WE'RE GETTING NEAR THE END OF THE ROAD for this visit. But I still have a couple of episodes I want to slip in. Life lived seemingly constantly on the road isn't like always being on vacation.

Both Jo's dad and my dad passed away a long while back. But both of our mothers were in failing health at the time Jo and I married. And both were in extended care facilities: Jo's mom in Brandon, my mom in Fulton. And their conditions were such that when we were in Brandon, we really needed to be in Fulton. And when we were in Fulton, we really needed to be in Brandon.

One weekend we had been to visit Mom in Fulton and needed to scurry back home. So we hit Highway 25 heading south and immediately fell in line the second car behind someone who was taking a leisurely drive home. The lead vehicle was doing about forty-five miles per hour and the car in front of me wouldn't pass him. And since there's only about a hundred yards where there is no double yellow line on that stretch of road between Fulton and Smithville, I never had the chance to get around both of them.

No matter how much I tailgated or shifted from side to side in my lane, neither of the drivers in front of me seemed to notice. Finally, the lead car turned, and I zipped around the fellow in front of me out of spite just as we were entering the Smithville city limits.

No sooner than we got around that car and straightened out, a big white car with two little old ladies pulled out in front of me from a side street. The driver was craning her neck to see over the dashboard. And I guess her foot couldn't reach the accelerator if she was sitting up high enough to see because she was only doing nineteen miles an hour! I glanced out my driver's side window at the perpetual double yellow line down the middle of the road. I looked at Jo and whined. Jo just shrugged.

And then, not that the little old ladies weren't going slow enough already, they stopped at the railroad track! I had had enough. There wasn't any traffic coming in the other lane, so I snarled out

POINT THE WAY. The roadway or the slit of light between the trees over it always leads the way home.

DOWNTOWN JACKSON. Just a reminder that not all of Mississippi is rural or rustic. Some is spectacularly modern.

NOVEMBER SUNSET. Face-time on TV or a lifetime out here? I think I made the right choice.

TENN-TOM AT FULTON. The waterway was so anticipated for so long that when it opened, my oldest aunt went every day and watched boats lock through at Fulton. Since 9/11, you can't do that anymore.

LOVE'S 1st STOP, TUTWILER. The Delta's original anthem, the blues, is kept authentic in places like this. Too authentic for Mama to have ever allowed me to go to.

LEVEE, DESOTO COUNTY. Books are yet to be written about how the levee changed the Delta from a swamp to the richest farmland on earth. And how the levee has managed to keep people in as much as it keeps water out, locked to the land.

something under my breath in French, whipped the wheel sharply to the left, gunned the engine, and zipped around them. Just as I was pulling back into my lane, I caught a glimpse of the Smithville police car on the side of the road. I thought I might have a chance of getting away with it, anyway, because there is always a police car parked on the side of the road in Smithville, and most of the time there is no one in it.

Not today, however. I peered in the rearview mirror and saw the patrol car ease out onto the road. He could have been going somewhere else, I thought. Then the blue lights came on. That sinking feeling hit me in the pit of my stomach. As I was pulling over to the shoulder, the two little old ladies putted by me and motored on down the road. I figured I'd have to pass them again before Amory after the policeman got through with me.

DRIVING DISTANCE. Jo and I ran across these signs while searching for Shubuta in Clark County. Wasn't it Steven Wright that said any place is within driving distance if you have the time?

SMITHVILLE. My brother Robert actually did get a ticket in Smithville late one night on his way home to Dad and Mom's in Fulton from his job at WKOR in Starkville, partly because his hair was too long. But it was in the early '70s, which is when most of the things really happened that we think we remember from the '60s. So I can see both points of view in light of the times. And Robert's present ability to grow long hair is just as much a distant memory.

Now, I know you are supposed to remain seated in your car when you are pulled over and wait for the officer to approach you. But the Smithville policeman was taking way too long, in my estimation, calling in my tag number or whatever, so I got out of my car and went back and stood beside his until he got out. Which he did pretty quickly when he looked up and saw me.

I started to explain to him that all I was trying to do was get home. That we had sick mamas at two ends of the state that needed to be checked on. And that we had already taken the scenic tour of Highway 25 from Fulton this far, and then the two little ladies pulled out in front of me and slowed me down even more.

As the officer pulled out his ticket pad, he explained to me that I had passed on a yellow line. To which I argued that I hadn't actually passed, I just went around them. He stopped writing momentarily and just looked at me. "Going around IS passing," he replied as his ballpoint regained motion.

"No it isn't," I reasoned, thinking at a speed that amazed me, anxiously waiting to hear what I was going to say next. "If they had been moving, I would have been passing them. But they were stopped for the railroad, so all I did was to go around them." I was impressed with myself. But he was still writing.

AMORY. Why wouldn't Hollywood want to come to Amory for the charity event "Stars Over Mississippi"? The downtown is so perfect it looks like a movie set.

"Lots of people stop for the railroad," the officer picked up. Then he paused his pen and looked at me and said, "Besides. I was sitting right there on the side of the road watching. What am I supposed to do?"

"Trust me," I answered. "If I had seen you sitting there on the side of the road, I would have never gone around them!" I think he laughed. Or at least smiled, or growled. All I know is he tore up the ticket and told me to go on home.

I'd hate to be a police officer and have to write tickets. I've never gotten a ticket at a convenient time. I seem to get them the day after the washing machine dies or when tuition is due for one of the kids or something. I would probably figure nobody else could afford a fine any more than I could and would give out way too many warnings to be profitable to the force.

Nevada Barr and I worked together on *Mississippi Roads* for a couple of seasons. She was still living in Clinton at the time and had most recently worked as a ranger on the Natchez Trace while researching the workings of the Trace for her mystery novels.

If you don't know, Nevada is this petite little thing. And if you've ever read any of her mysteries, then you know that no one ever just gets cleanly shot or stabbed in them. No! They are disemboweled by crazed bears or picked to death by buzzards and the like. Not to mention the cussing!

I asked her one time where she came up with all of that stuff. "Oh, I'm venting," she smiled. "You wouldn't believe how many of my former co-workers I've killed off in my books!"

Another time when we were talking about her being a ranger on the Trace, Nevada told me that late one night she stopped a matronly lady for speeding. I can't remember whether she gave her a ticket or a warning, but as she was walking back to her patrol car, the lady asked her, "Darlin'? Aren't you afraid to be out here all by yourself late at night like this?" To which Nevada patted her side and answered, "I've got my pistol with me." To which the woman replied, "Why, don't we ALL?"

NEVADA BARR AND ME. I hope I am never a model for a character that gets ripped to shreds in one of Nevada's mysteries. I'm more the handsome, hero type, don't you think? (Hey! Go with me here. We're talking fiction!)

GERMAN BAPTIST, SMITH COUNTY. The small community of Amish-like believers doesn't use cars or electricity or cell phones or anything modern at all. You may feel sorry for them. But three dollars-plus a gallon at the pump doesn't worry them in the least bit.

The late afternoon sun was shining directly into my face through the windshield by the time I left the tiny town of Paulding in Jasper County, heading back home after shooting a story there. Paulding was once known as the Queen City of the East. That was back before the Civil War. There is still an active courthouse there. Jasper is one of those counties with two county seats, Paulding and Bay Springs. But the present-day building is the third courthouse in Paulding. The first two burned. The original courthouse was supposed to have been the only two-story structure between New Orleans and Chattanooga at the time. The one there now is a flat building that doesn't even attempt to reflect any of the grandeur of its predecessors.

Paulding still has a couple of old store buildings and a few houses, but that's about it. The 150-year-old jail is still standing, but you may have to fight off rattlesnakes to hack through the bushes to get to it nowadays.

As I drove westward from Paulding toward home, the sun was so low that it would set as I followed the road down from the hilltops into the valleys. Then as I'd continue up to the top of the next ridge, it would rise again. I'm sure I'd seen this rising/setting phenomenon before, but that day it just caught my attention. A week's worth of sunrises and sunsets over the course of a few miles. After a while of this, I topped a hill and the sun didn't come all the way back up. Then at the top of the next hill, it didn't come back up at all. There was only a bright glow on the horizon where it had set for good for the day.

HATTIESBURG SAENGER THEATRE. Here's one of those treasures at the end of the rainbow, or at least at the end of a drive to do another story. The old art deco theatre has been completely restored, right down to the pipe organ.

ETHEL CAFÉ. The cash register quit singing at Joe Joe's a long time ago. The 10-2-4 sign below is an advertisement for Dr Pepper. Is the faded figure in the middle the good doctor? Signs of the times.

TREE TUNNEL. It's like you're driving in story land when you go through some of the scenery on the Trace. But the 50 mph speed limit and a pistol packin' ranger will bring you back to reality quickly. So watch it.

PAULDING. We're still a relatively new nation as far as the span of civilization goes. So we don't know exactly how long we should expect for our Queen Cities to rise, peak, plateau, and vanish. Paulding did it in less than a half century. That may be a record.

It was late summer, but the evening was mild enough that I turned off the air-conditioner and rolled down the windows. There must have been a billion katydids. They were in every tree for miles at a stretch. Their rising and falling chirping in unison seemed to stay right beside me as I drove as if I weren't moving at all.

The highway sounded as if it had just rained, the asphalt had heated so much from the broiling sun all day. A warm puff of air would blow through my open window, then a cooler one as night was starting to come on.

Smells you only get whiffs of with your car windows rolled up envelop you with them rolled down. There is a sharp dankness in creek bottoms. The woods have a spicy aroma, sweetened by pines in places. Chicken houses must smell like money to the owners who live next to them, less so to us who hurry by them as quickly as we can.

LAST GLOW OF DAY. No matter how many hilltops, the sun finally sets.

BOYKIN FACILITY. That's the problem with one-room church houses like Boykin Church in Smith County. You really need to have at least one or two other rooms down in the woods somewhere. Boykin was modern for its times. It had two rooms. Here's the ladies.

People who work in Laurel or Hattiesburg or Meridian or Jackson and live here in the country were just getting home for the evening about that time. Cars turning into driveways or onto gravel roads leading to driveways back in the woods somewhere thinned the traffic on the main highway regularly as I drove on, leaving me more and more by myself.

Twilight deepened as miles of the roadway passed from in front of to behind me. The sky repainted itself in the west as I went, changing from orange to shades of pink, then purple, and finally to gray. Yard lights flickered on. Kitchen lights and living room lights stood out from the fading silhouettes of their houses, glowing faintly at first, then brighter, and casting projected trapezoidal shapes of themselves on the yards beneath them as the evening settled in.

The trees in the woods along the road eventually gave up their individuality as the light faded and they darkened into one single shadow like chocolate chips melting together in a boiler. I could see where the road was going by looking up above at the gray opening between the blackness of the trees on either side of the road, forming an elongated "V" between the shadows on the right and the shadows on the left, forming an arrow that pointed me onward. The outlines of the houses became indistinguishable as darkness fell, and after a while it seemed that the blackness of the trees along either side of the road had lighted windows cut into it.

A little feeling of melancholy falls over me sometimes when I drive from daylight into darkness and I am not yet home. It doesn't usually last long, especially if the moon rises. The moon is great company while driving at night.

I do start to feel like a nomad or something, sometimes.

THE EDGE OF NIGHT. The sky is still light but the world at ground level has already slipped into night mode as trees melt together and people toddle into their homes.

MOON AND CHURCH. I've had no telling how many wearisome drives home after dark instantly transformed into a delightful experience simply by the moon rising.

SULLIVAN'S HOLLOW a hundred years ago was no place for a stranger, especially after dark. Now, I don't think the folks there ever meet a stranger. And the rolling landscape is beautiful.

AND IF ELECTED… I promise not to accept. I don't have any idea who came up with the idea for me to be governor. But I like it the way it is. He wishes he had MY job!

(I would say gypsy, but I'm not that flashy.) A constant traveler, let's put it. Sundown is time to be home. Yet here I was still on the road with miles and miles to go, as I had been countless other sundowns before and have been countless others since then. I sort of envied the people whose homes I was passing, already settling in after the day's work, supper on the table. Being in the place that is theirs. There is a satisfactory completeness to the idea of such a thing.

When I was a kid, we had a sand pile we played in. We created perfect worlds there. We'd use the sides of our hands as road graders and make a network of streets and highways and then use matchboxes or anything else as houses and barns and stores. And we'd work on our little towns or homesteads until we had them just right. It was so pleasing to see what we'd made and how well we could make it function. I imagined all those homesteads I was passing that night were as pleasing to their owners in real life as our pretend ones had been to us in our sand pile.

I have a home at the end of my drive, too. But I was still a good distance away. At that moment, I was one of the world's wanderers: nothing to hold me down; free to roam. While driving, I thought back over that day. I had been to the former Queen City of the East. I'd graze the upper end of Sullivan's Hollow in a few miles. And before I got home, I'd be driving where Civil War battles had been fought. On top of that, I had just seen a bunch of sunrises and sunsets in a matter of minutes, and I still had nighttime and the stars, the moon, and the fireflies yet to go before I got to my house.

People everywhere say they want my job because I get to go to so many places and see so many things. I remind them of the deadlines that go along with all that traveling and how sometimes it becomes a matter of not so much GETTING to go, but HAVING to go to those all those places.

But the destinations are going to be the same, whether I'm approaching the trip as getting to go or having to go. It's the attitude that's the difference. I can make it drudgery or delight. It's all up to me. And the traveling is really a delight now that I'm free to go and I am not constrained by having to hold fort at the weather set at the TV station doing something like waiting for a forecast update to render on a computer model.

Closer to home, all the roads grow very familiar. To go anywhere, I have to travel one of these roads to get from my house first, no matter which connecting highways I take farther into the journey. And as I come in from where I've been, all these churches, old homes, fields, and stores become my mile markers. I know how far in minutes I am from my house when I drive by each one because I've passed these landmarks so many times before.

And once I get home, I know I won't be there for long; just time enough to copy the video I've shot that day into the computer, write the story to go along with it, edit it all together, air it, and then get out the maps and the GPS and head out again.

I know there will come a day when we can't do all this traveling. So that's why Jo and I try to enjoy every mile of it as we go, and overlook gas prices and slow traffic and try not to think about the things at the house that we need to be doing. Because for a while longer at least, we also have a home on the road. And there are still lots of places to go and more people to meet and stories to tell before we have to park the car for good.

SUN DIAL. Time moves so slowly when you are watching it, like the sun's shadow across the face of a sundial. But it only takes from sunup until sundown every day to do it. That's quick and slow at the same time.

COMFORTS OF HOME. The sun is sinking and you still have a long way to go to get home, and then you see the EPA lines laced over the countryside and remember that bright lights and all the modern conveniences are just a few more miles away.

SHACK UP INN, CLARKSDALE. Billed as Mississippi's first B&B: bed and beer. The owners salvaged the tenant houses from surrounding plantations and intended to open a bed and breakfast but realized nobody wanted to get up and cook. So they improvised.

ABOUT THE AUTHOR

Walt Grayson is a native Mississippian, having grown up in Greenville, where he met his wife, Jo, in junior high school. His love for travel may have stemmed from often going to work with his dad. His job took him up and down the roads of the Delta every day, and Walt never grew tired of the adventures of the miles.

Walt says the idea of "writers" is something that was drilled into students in the Greenville school system because of all the writers from the Delta, in general, and Greenville, in particular, living there at that time.

But his love for storytelling came from listening to tales told after supper around the fireplace in his grandmother's living room during family gatherings. Stories about the way things were a long time ago, and notable incidents (some funny, some sad) involving acquaintances.

His love for photography also comes from family roots. There were boxes and boxes of family photographs in his home when he was a child, and Walt would entertain himself perusing through them on rainy days.

In this book, his love for storytelling and writing is combined with his photography to bring us tales from his home state, Mississippi. And even Jo, his first true love, is along with him for many of the adventures.